INTRODUCTION

Welcome to the So Connected® Mental Strength Coaching Journal.

Do you ever feel like your mind and body are not on the same page? Do you over-think things or get stuck in your head? Do you know *what* to do, but it doesn't always turn out right?

The purpose of this journal is to give you the strategies and tools you need to be your best. As you learn, practice, and process, you will create more success, eliminate old issues, and achieve better results.

Putting more of *you* into *your* life is a practice.

I can't wait to see what you do with it!

— Stacey

Copyright © 2020 by Stacey Herman Goodrich
All rights reserved. This book or any portion thereof
may not be reproduced or used in any manner
without the express written permission of the author
except for the use of brief quotations in a book review.

ISBN: 978-1-7354571-0-9

Printed in the United States of America

Designed by Kirstie Walheim
www.hellboxbooks.com

JOIN THE GROUP

Please join my Facebook group:
Mental Strength Coaching Journal For Athletes

It's for you, the person using this journal. Ask me questions, talk with others on the same journey, and surround yourself with support.

Additional Facebook group support:
Athletes Who Settle For More

Social Media:
www.so-connected.com
@staceyhermangoodrich
@ConnectedStacey
Athletes Who Settle For More

THIS BOOK BELONGS TO:

_____

Who I am is perfect, but what I do will always be up for judgment.
I will focus on what I can control, and do away with what doesn't serve me.
I will practice, adjust, and enjoy the journey.

TABLE OF *Contents*

3 — INTRODUCTION

5 — JOIN THE GROUP

9 — SNAPSHOT OF THE PROCESS

11 — THE PROCESS

11 — STEP 1: CHOOSE YOUR INTENTIONAL WORD OF THE DAY

14 — STEP 2: THE STRATEGIES – PRACTICING YOUR SUCCESS

15 — THE DOING STRATEGY®

17 — THE LEARNING STRATEGY®

18 — A-CIRCLE STRATEGY®

22 — STEP 3: GOALS IN MOTION

22 — GOAL BEYOND THE GOAL®

24 — STEP 4: PURGE IT. VENT. GET IT OUT!

26 — 1ST MONTH JOURNALING SECTION

98 — 2ND MONTH JOURNALING SECTION

170 — 3RD MONTH JOURNALING SECTION

243 — STICKER PAGE

STRATEGIES ARE WHAT YOU CAN DUPLICATE TO BE MORE SUCCESSFUL.

© Stacey Herman Goodrich

SNAPSHOT OF THE PROCESS

1 INTENTIONAL WORD OF THE DAY

Work your mindset daily! Pick a word or phrase that you connect with. Use the intentional word of the day to reset your mentality. It keeps you intentional in the moment and gives you the choice to be in charge. Focus on where you want to be!

2 THE STRATEGIES –PRACTICING YOUR SUCCESS

Doing Strategy®, **Learning** Strategy®, and **A-Circle**® O! Strategies give you the *how* —how to duplicate success and perform in your potential over time.

3 GOALS IN MOTION

Small daily goals align your mind and body. A **Goal Beyond The Goal**® will give you purpose (the why) of your day-to-day responsibilities. Over time your results show your success.

4 PURGE IT ALL! GET IT OUT!

Purge it all! Get it out! As you do –replace it with what you want now! Let's dig in!

GIVE YOURSELF PERMISSION TO NOT BE PERFECT SO YOU CAN BECOME MORE EXCELLENT!

© Stacey Herman Goodrich

THE PROCESS

STEP 1 CHOOSE YOUR INTENTIONAL WORD OF THE DAY

Pick a word or phrase that connects to you… each day. Pick one listed on the next page or one of your own! The ability to control your mindset, in the moment, is important. We can all be affected by our situations; this strategy keeps us focused.

Here is an example of how to use the Intentional Word Of The Day. Let's use the phrase, "fresh start." Imagine you are a player on a softball team, and a teammate has an at-bat that isn't positive, you could say, "fresh start!"

This resets your teammate's mentality. It stops the negative thoughts and actions, and allows them to choose to change it! It's a way to practice adjusting perspective in the moment. Does that make sense? Resetting your mentality with an intentional word of the day puts you in charge. It gives you power over the moment.

Your present situation may be stressful or chaotic, but choosing to shift your thoughts to your goals can help. Think of it as separating your "present self" from your "goal self." In the moment, you can decide to focus on what you need to do to move toward your goals instead of being caught up in the annoyance of your situation. The Intentional Word Of The Day can keep you connected to your goals, even in a moment of distress.

Practicing this strategy on a day-to-day basis allows us to be in charge of our situation, choose our behaviors and thoughts, and can help us be more successful over time. This journal gives you the ability to acknowledge it, track it, and get better at it!

SUGGESTIONS FOR THE WORD OF THE DAY

Below are words that you can use, but feel free to use whatever word works for you on a day-to-day basis.

When you affirm words it is helpful, but intentionally connecting words to your behavior is EMPOWERING YOUR POWER!

I suggest you do this personally and add it to your team to bring more success.

WORD SUGGESTIONS

Connected	Faith	Commitment
Movement	Fearless	Mindset
Goal	Drive	Motivation
Knowledgeable	Abundance	Accomplish
Accountability	Graceful	Refined
Choice	Meaningful	Fresh Start
Express	Happy	Open-minded
Belief	Opportunity	Creative
Captivate	Healthy	Positivity
Optimism	Thankful	Strength
Legacy	Illuminate	Harmony
Support	Attitude	Thoughtful
Determination	Joy	Grateful
Genuine	Intention	Wisdom
Love	Excellent	Leadership
Essence	Kindness	Mentally Strong
Openhearted	Eager	Acceptance
Extraordinary	Legendary	Grit
Togetherness	Fabulous	Strategies

WHEN YOU AFFIRM WORDS IT IS HELPFUL, BUT INTENTIONALLY CONNECTING WORDS TO YOUR BEHAVIOR IS *EMPOWERING* *YOUR POWER*

© Stacey Herman Goodrich

STEP 2 THE STRATEGIES – PRACTICING YOUR SUCCESS

Everybody has strategies. Strategies are used to be successful or unsuccessful, to get what we want, or what we don't want. A common problem is that most people are unaware of the strategy they are using, therefore, they cannot control their outcomes consistently. Strategies are happening at the unconscious level or automatically.

Is it frustrating for you when you know what to do to be successful, but it doesn't turn out the way you want? Have you practiced the skill/play/game enough to provide success, but the result is still lacking?

The **Doing Strategy**®, the **Learning Strategy**®, and **A-Circle**® are strategies that will give you options to manage situations better. Learning and understanding these strategies will help you get the results you want.

IF JUST TELLING YOU TO BE CONFIDENT, NOT TO WORRY ABOUT IT, TO GET OUT OF YOUR HEAD, WORKED — WE WOULD ALL BE PERFECT.

© Stacey Herman Goodrich

DOING STRATEGY®

THE DOING STRATEGY® IS WHEN YOUR MIND IS NOT IN YOUR WAY, YOUR BODY KNOWS WHAT TO DO, AND YOU CAN JUST DO IT.

When you first started practicing your sport, you didn't have to think about what you were doing, you just did it! You picked up a ball and threw it (maybe not accurately), you did a cartwheel (maybe not perfectly), you jumped in the pool to swim (maybe not gracefully).

Most people "do" their skills/plays/game for many years but it's happening automatically, so consciously they are unable to use its potential. At this point, because it is an unconscious strategy, when something goes wrong, they don't know what to do or how to fix it.

I had a client who played football, and he said to me, "I can kick a football straight through the upright over and over again in practice, but when I get to a game, or a pressure situation, I can't do it." His coaches would keep saying, "Don't worry about it, just get out of your head."

If telling people, "don't worry about it, just get out of your head" or "just be confident you can do it" worked, we would all be perfectly consistent, right?

For my client, the football athlete (I will call him Joe), when he was practicing, he was basically just doing it. He just kicked the ball and didn't really have to think about it. Then in a game, or pressure situation, just doing it didn't work. When this happened Joe did not know what to do. Typically when just "doing it" doesn't work for people, it is common for them to mentally bail out and get stuck.

I told Joe, "If you can just do your skills/game (kicks) **without a lot of thought**, that is an option. That is the Doing Strategy®."

Bringing awareness to what was working for him in the past ("doing" his kick), giving it a name (the Doing Strategy®), allows him to consider it (I have an option), practice it (I am going to just do my skill without a lot of thought), and maximize its potential (owning it!)

Understanding the Doing Strategy® provides a mental connection to what to do physically **in the moment.** This is an option, and a solution.

Where in the past did you just do your skills/plays/game? Can you now see where you could have used the Doing Strategy®? Can you see how when moving forward you can just do your skills without much thought? In this journal, you will be able to practice this idea to support yourself.

Typically, with athletes, there is a situation where just "doing it" doesn't work. It could be when you are on a new/better team and you're worried about what the coach is thinking, or you have a high expectation of yourself and that idea gets in your way, preventing you from doing what you want. For Joe, it was the pressure situation where just "doing it" did not work. He needed another option. I taught him the Learning Strategy®.

DOING STRATEGY® IS JUST DOING IT WITHOUT A LOT OF THOUGHT.

© Stacey Herman Goodrich

LEARNING STRATEGY® KEEPS YOUR MIND CONNECTED TO YOUR BODY.

© Stacey Herman Goodrich

LEARNING STRATEGY®

THE LEARNING STRATEGY® IS FOCUSING ON YOUR SKILL/PLAY/GAME ONE PIECE AT A TIME OR HOW YOU ARE DOING IT IN THE MOMENT.

The Learning Strategy® is focusing on your skill/play/game one piece at a time, or how you are doing it in the moment. It is not thinking about what you *need* to do, and then trying to do it. It is thinking about what you *want* to do, **as you are doing it.**

When I taught this strategy to Joe, I said, "Joe, when you are kicking the ball in practice, what are you thinking about?" He said, "Nothing, I am just doing it." I said, "Okay, when you are kicking the ball in practice, what do you want to be focusing on so that when you kick in the game, you are mentally prepared?" He said, "I want to focus on how I connect my foot to the ball, my technique, and my follow-through." I said, "Great. Can you practice it that way so when you are in a game you are mentally ready?" He said, "Yes."

The Learning Strategy® is focusing on your technique, form, or mechanics. It is thinking about HOW you want to do it physically. It keeps your mind connected to your body, supporting what you are doing, AS YOU ARE DOING IT.

Do you ever feel like your mind and your body are not on the same page? Do you ever have negative thoughts controlling you?

When things don't go right, negative thoughts can get in our way. If we do not give our mind a job to do, it can create its own job, and sometimes it might not be helpful. Sometimes our mind might be thinking about what we don't want to happen, what we are worried about, or what our coaches are thinking. Unfortunately, this disconnects our mind from our body, causing us issues physically.

The Learning Strategy® gives your mind a job to focus on, **what you want,** instead of what you do not want to happen. It's a strategy that connects your mind to your body.

Think back to situations that did not go well for you. Do you see how using the Learning Strategy® could have been helpful, — a way you could have approached it one step at a time? In this journal we will explore this, and work with it, to help you create more success.

A-CIRCLE STRATEGY®

A-CIRCLE® PROVIDES US THE CAPABILITY TO BE AWARE OF WHAT IS CONTROLLING US, AND GIVES US THE ABILITY TO MANAGE IT.

Many times we have situations where what is controlling us is not what we want. Sometimes negative thoughts, limiting beliefs, and anxiety/pressure/stress can be running the show. It is difficult because obviously we don't want this, but again it is happening unconsciously. Have you ever had a coach tell you, "get out of your head," or "you are over-thinking it"? Just because the coach did not have a solution for you, doesn't mean there isn't one. **There is nothing wrong with your mind and you are not the problem.** A-Circle® provides us the capability to be aware of what is controlling us, and gives us the ability to manage it.

Everyone has a mental A Circle, B Circle, and C Circle. (See diagram on page 19)

A Circle: Whoever or whatever is in your A Circle is who or what is making decisions for you, or who or what is running the show for you in that particular situation.

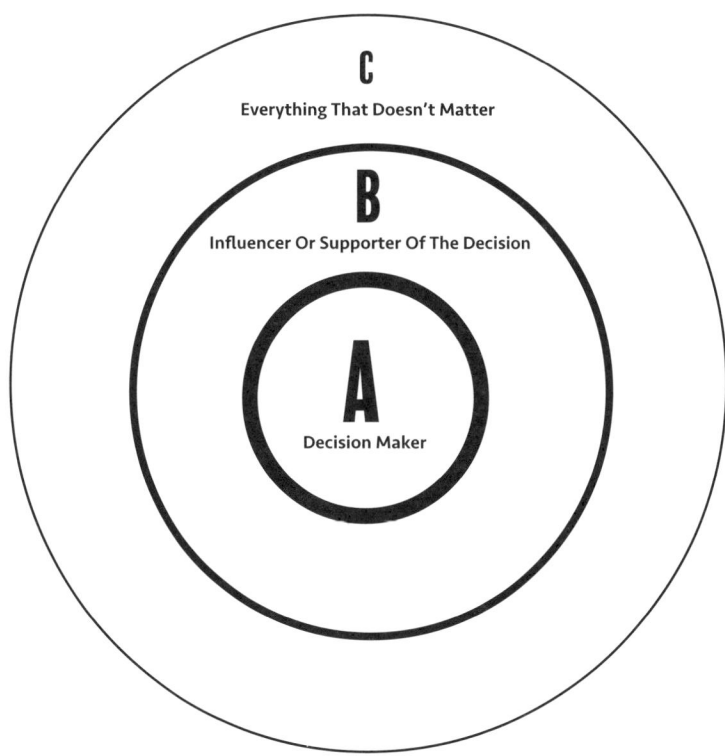

Diagram of A-CIRCLE STRATEGY®
© Stacey Herman Goodrich

A CIRCLE

Who or what is making decisions for you, or who or what is running the show for you in that particular situation.

B CIRCLE

People or things that influence your decisions, or they can support you to make a decision, but they're not actually making it for you.

C CIRCLE

Everyone and everything outside of your A and B Circle, or everything that doesn't matter or is irrelevant.

B Circle: Contains people or things that influence your decisions, or they can support you to make a decision, but they're not actually making it for you.

C Circle: Contains everyone and everything outside of your A and B Circle, or everything that doesn't matter or is irrelevant.

We can have lots of things in our A Circle —we can have people, thoughts, energy. You may have your coaches, family, and/or teammates in your A Circle in certain situations. You may or may not be in your own A Circle at times. Do you worry about making a mistake, or what people think of you? These ideas could be in your A Circle and controlling you at times, correct? Do you play well in practice, but in a game, pressure jumps into your A Circle? —similar to Joe's situation. Have you experienced a time when worry, anxiety, or injury were in your A Circle? Do you see how in those situations it was controlling you?

We can also manage what we want in our A Circle. We can kick everything out, and just do our skills (the Doing Strategy®), we can focus on one thing at a time (the Learning Strategy®), we can have confidence, people who support us, and belief in ourselves, in our A Circle.

The same day that I taught Joe the Doing Strategy® and the Learning Strategy®, I taught him A-Circle®. I said to him, "Joe, everybody has an A Circle, B Circle, and C Circle. There is no right or wrong way with how it is set up. It is a way for us to understand what's running the show in any given situation. Whoever or whatever is in your A Circle is who or what is making decisions for you. Your B Circle contains people or things that influence your decisions, or they can support you to make a decision, but they're not making it for you.
C Circle contains everything else outside of that —everything else irrelevant."

I asked Joe, "When you think back to the game where you couldn't kick the ball correctly, what was in your A Circle?" He said, "I was worried that I was going to mess up." I said to him, "Do you see how that idea was controlling you?" He said, "Yes." I said, "In that situation, what could you have had in your A Circle?" He said, "I could have just been focusing on how I needed to kick the ball." I said, "Do you see how that would have been different for you?" He said, "Yes."

Think back to a situation in your sport that didn't go well. Who or what was in your A Circle? What could you have had in your A Circle back then? Moving forward, what do you want to have in your A Circle?

These are some of the questions we will process throughout this journal. Do not worry if you do not understand every bit of this right now. This journal will help you practice gently, but effectively. Give yourself permission to not be perfect, so over time you can be your best in your sport, school, and whatever else you choose to take on.

WHAT'S IN YOUR A CIRCLE?

STEP 3 GOALS IN MOTION

Now that you have learned the strategies (ways you can manage your situations and your game) let's talk about goals. Goals are great! When you think of your goals do they get you excited? Do you feel pressure? Both? In this journal you will practice maximizing your ability to set and reach your goals.

GOAL BEYOND THE GOAL®

People can feel stuck, unmotivated, or be worried about a result. These are common issues when it comes to the mental side of the sport. A solution to these issues is having a goal beyond a goal.

Goal Beyond The Goal® is a strategy used to keep people mentally focused on what they want to do in the moment, to support their desired outcome. For example, I was working with a basketball player (I will call her Addison), who would always hesitate when she shot the basket, but she wanted to make more shots. She was worried about making a mistake, and did not want to be taken out of the game. When she would go up for a shot, she would tend to pass it off, or miss. She was mentally distracted or disconnected from her body because of those thoughts.

Addison had worry in her A Circle and it was controlling her. I asked her, "Addison, what do you want to have in your A Circle when you are shooting?" She said, "My form and how I shoot." Then I asked, "After you make the shot, then what do you want to be focusing on?" She said, "Defense and getting the ball back."

Acknowledging what was in her A Circle (worry and negative thoughts), replacing that with what she wanted in her A Circle (her form and technique), keeps her mind connected to her body. Giving her a new place to land (getting the ball back/defense), assures that she can stay connected through the process.

Without a new place to land (defense or getting the ball back), beyond the desired outcome (making the shot), people tend to mentally leave their body or bail out. It's important to have a Goal Beyond The Goal® mentality throughout your day to keep you moving forward toward your bigger goals. This will help you stay aligned with your behavior to achieve what you want daily.

Whenever you feel stagnant or unmotivated, use this strategy to support your process. If you're frustrated because you can't get a skill, focus on what you want to be doing after you learn the skill. It creates a window to move through, instead of a door that you're pounding your head against. Example: How do I want to hit the ball so that I can get to first base? Or what do I need to focus on while doing my giant to help me move into my flyaway?

Long-term Goal Beyond The Goal® mentality helps you understand how everything that you are going through now, easy or hard, is supporting what you want for yourself, in your future. For example, if I ask an athlete, "What is your goal in three years?" And they say, "To be in the Olympics." What we are doing is taking a snapshot of where they want to be three years down the road, throwing it into their time-line and dropping it down. **This aligns the athlete with what they want for themselves in the future, today.**

Moving forward, everything that they are doing today is helping them prepare to be successful for the Olympics tomorrow. Looking at it from this perspective gives them the ability to continue moving forward even on the rough days. It keeps their mentality **in the process** instead of worrying about every single daily result or outcome.

Think about where you want to be three years down the road. In this journal you will work toward all of your goals effectively, efficiently, and successfully.

STEP 4 PURGE IT. VENT. GET IT OUT!

Purge everything that you're thinking about, get it out. If you have an opportunity to vent do it, but make sure the person you're venting to understands that *you don't need to be fixed*. You're not broken and they don't need to interject themselves into your A Circle. You just want to talk and *get it out*!

Or —journal it. Acknowledging your feelings and writing them down is important. Once you move through the problem you will see more of the solution. Getting to the root of the problem is essential because that's where your solution lies.

After you get through the issues that you are feeling or experiencing —then what? Now what do you want to do? How do you want to use your situation to build on, to create more, and to be better because of it? For example, think about the one thing today that is completely bothering you. Now I want you to turn it around and be grateful for it. This is another opportunity to journal.

Experience the feelings that you are having; maybe you feel them in your body. If so, what part of your body? You can use color as well to express what's going on inside. Also, you may need to hear yourself process —just go on a walk and talk yourself through some things that you are experiencing or feeling. Practice taking your judgment of yourself out of your A Circle. The more accepting you can be of yourself, the more success you will have in becoming all that you want to be! Be gentle with yourself, but go after it!

YOU'RE READY TO DO THE WORK!

TRUST THE PROCESS.

MONTH _____ 20 _____

MONDAY	TUESDAY	WEDNESDAY	THURSDAY

NOBODY DOES *YOU* IN YOUR SPORT BETTER THAN YOU.
BE CONFIDENT IN THAT.

© Stacey Herman Goodrich

FRIDAY	SATURDAY	SUNDAY

MONDAY DAILY JOURNALING   DATE _____

MENTAL MINDSET FOR THE WEEK

Welcome! This is all about you. This week it is important to be open. Consider the strategies and goals. Practice being mentally strong!

JOURNALING PROMPTS

- Pick your intentional word or phrase of the day.

  _____

- Think about the past, what strategies did you use? The Doing Strategy®? The Learning Strategy®? Combination? Both? Neither?

- Think about what went well and what did not go well in the past. What strategies were you using in those situations? What was in your A Circle?

- Where do you see yourself in 3 years? You can always change your mind, but think big, think boldly, just explore in lots of different areas of your life.

- Think about your past — what has been in the way of you being successful? Purge it, write without judgment, move through these things so beyond it you can see the opportunity. Write about the opportunity beyond the struggle.

- Now look at all these things that were in your way. Turn each one around and decide how you can be grateful for each.

TUESDAY DAILY JOURNALING   DATE _____

JOURNALING PROMPTS

○ Pick your intentional word or phrase of the day.
_____

○ How did yesterday's intentional word of the day or phrase support you?
_____
_____
_____

○ How did you use the Doing Strategy®, Learning Strategy®, and A-Circle®?
_____
_____
_____
_____

○ Name a couple of examples where now looking back, you were able to use the strategies to move toward your goal.
_____
_____
_____
_____
_____

○ What went well yesterday?
_____
_____
_____

○ Think about the strategy you were using to do that well? What was it?
_____
_____
_____

- Where can you practice that same strategy moving forward?

- How can this strategy help you achieve your goal in the next 3 months?

- Lets talk about difficult situations. Write down examples of situations for you where you felt victimized, or you felt bad, maybe something or someone that made you feel terrible. Just write things down and get them out.

- In these situations what was in your A Circle?

- Now looking back, think about how you could have supported yourself, or taken care of yourself better. What could you have had in your A Circle to support you?

- What inspired you today?

WEDNESDAY DAILY JOURNALING   DATE _____

JOURNALING PROMPTS

- Pick your intentional word or phrase of the day.
  _____

- How did yesterday's intentional word of the day or phrase support you and shift your mentality?
  _____
  _____

- This week, can you think of examples where you were able to just "do" your skills/game/sport? The Doing Strategy®?
  _____
  _____
  _____

- When you think of the Learning Strategy®, do you like to see your way through your skills/plays/sport? Feel your way through? Talk your way through? Think your way through? Or a combination? Think of a skill/play/situation where you can practice it. What do you want to be focusing on?
  _____
  _____
  _____

- Can you practice using this strategy moving forward? Where?
  _____
  _____
  _____

- Think of a time in your past where you felt confident. Explain your experience.
  _____
  _____
  _____

- When you think back to that experience, go back INTO that experience. Now, as you step out of it, how were you confident? Was it something you felt, something you saw, something you said to yourself, something you heard, or a combination?

  _____
  _____
  _____

- Can you practice this strategy moving forward to be more confident?

  _____
  _____

- Think about experiences for you in the past where you were confident. What was in your A Circle?

  _____
  _____

- Remember, your goal is seeking you as much as you are seeking it. Name 3 things that you have been working on this week that are moving you toward your goal.

  _____
  _____
  _____

- Think about your situation. What are some great things about your situation (coaches, team, parents, club/school) that can support you to achieve your goals?

  _____
  _____
  _____
  _____

- Now as you are more aware of these resources, how can you use them more to support you?

  _____
  _____
  _____

THURSDAY DAILY JOURNALING   DATE _____

JOURNALING PROMPTS

- Pick your intentional word or phrase of the day. Pick something that keeps you aligned with your "goal self." _____

- Remember that you have a "present self" and a "goal self." Practice stepping out of your "present self" and stepping into your "goal self" more often. Where have you done that? Where can you do it more?

  _____
  _____
  _____
  _____

- Do you have situations where your A Circle gets crowded with negative thoughts or negative energy or negative people? Are you having trouble kicking them out? If you are struggling with negative things in your A Circle, remember that they were once there for a good reason. So think of a situation where something negative would not leave your A Circle. Now ask yourself what that good reason was that it was there in the first place.

  _____
  _____
  _____
  _____

- An example: if you have fear/anxiety/worry in your A Circle, it is only there to help you pay attention, think about what you want to be doing, or reminding you to focus on what you are doing physically. Practice thanking that energy (yes thanking) so you can use it to your advantage. Think of old situations and practice doing this. What could you have done to support you better in the past?

  _____
  _____
  _____
  _____

- Think of some goals outside of your sport that you want to achieve. What are they?

  _____
  _____
  _____
  _____

- Can you see how these tools and strategies can support you to achieve them? How?

  _____
  _____
  _____
  _____

- Can you see how you can use these tools and strategies to support your team? You do not have to do anything extra other than recognize where your teammates are more connected mentally. Acknowledge that for them —that acknowledgment will come back to support you as well. Where could you have done this in the past?

  _____
  _____
  _____
  _____
  _____

- You can only see in others what you have in yourself. If it is negative, consider working on your own reflection. What are you reflecting out into the world? Where are you not showing up for yourself? How do you want to change that?

  _____
  _____
  _____
  _____
  _____

FRIDAY DAILY JOURNALING   DATE _____

JOURNALING PROMPTS

- Pick your intentional word or phrase of the day. Think about your week. What can you focus on today that will support your entire week?

- Can you think of situations this week where you were more in your own A Circle?

- How was that helpful for you?

- When you think about your A Circle, can you see how your managing of it can be helpful for your goals? What did you learn this week about how you are able to manage your A Circle?

- Think of situations in the past that did not go well. An injury? Maybe you broke down under pressure, or you were worried about what people were thinking of you. Write them down.

- Looking back, do you see that if you would have known these tools and strategies, they would have been helpful? Remember, you did the best you could with what you knew at the time. What strategies could you have used? What could you have had in your A Circle?

    _____
    _____
    _____
    _____
    _____

- This week, when you look back, name 3 reasons for your success.

    _____
    _____
    _____
    _____

- What do you do well? How do you do it well? Remember: nobody does your skills/sport/game better than you —be confident in that.

    _____
    _____
    _____
    _____
    _____
    _____

- Step back and practice joy. Where do you have the most joy in your life? Do more of that.

    _____
    _____
    _____
    _____
    _____
    _____

I AM SO PROUD OF YOU!

SATURDAY DAILY JOURNALING DATE _____

CELEBRATION DAY!

- Think of 5 situations where you were successful. Write them down.

_____
_____
_____
_____
_____
_____

- Think of 5 things that you accomplished this week. Write them down.

_____
_____
_____
_____
_____
_____

- Where did you build strength this week mentally? Physically?

_____
_____
_____
_____
_____
_____

- What did you learn from this week that can support you to achieve your goals?

_____
_____
_____
_____
_____
_____

- What went well? What didn't go well? And what can you learn from both?

___

- Remember that you are not equal to the result. When you accomplish a goal, it is fantastic —*but you are not equal to it.* Learn from it so you can use that experience and same strategy to build success. Where this week can you use this?

___

- Also, you are not equal to the mistake, or what did not go well. Separate yourself from those situations so that you can also learn from them. Can you think of any situation this week where you can practice this? Are you hard on yourself? Do you have high expectations of yourself? That's okay, but neither of those things belong in your A Circle when you are doing your sport. Did you have situations this week where this got in your way?

SUNDAY! DAILY JOURNALING   DATE _____

DREAM DAY!

○ Give yourself permission to dream. We need to practice dreaming. It's not a bad thing to desire, or to want things in your life! Putting your best self into your life, sharing your gift to the world, being more of you, is your responsibility and your job. Dreaming only inspires more of you in that way. As you practice putting more of you into your life, you can share that with others; that is inspiring. Where this week were you more of you?

_____
_____
_____
_____
_____

○ Regarding your answer above, were people receptive to it or a little bit threatened?

_____
_____
_____

Remember this: I can only see in you what I have in myself. So, if I don't see you in all your brightness, it's not because something is wrong with you. It is my lack that is the issue. Do not let someone else's inability to see your light dim it. Practice being your light. Practice seeing other's light as well.

○ Practice these 5 mindset rules:
1. Set big, bold, tremendous goals.
2. Be grateful for everything you have today, and everything you don't have yet.
3. Be 100% accountable for your life. It doesn't mean that everything is your fault, but taking 100% responsibility for it moves you forward with strength.
4. Be thankful – for everything that went well and for everything that didn't go well.
5. Act, speak, think, and perform from the perspective of your Goal Beyond The Goal®.

Practice these mindset rules EVERY day.

MONDAY DAILY JOURNALING   DATE _____

MENTAL MINDSET FOR THE WEEK

Congratulations! You've made it a week! Have you joined the Facebook group: Mental Strength Coaching Journal, yet? This week be open to gentle and effective change. As you become more aware of your A Circle, you can practice to be your best.

JOURNALING PROMPTS

○ Pick your intentional word or phrase of the day.
_____

○ Think about the past, what strategies did you use? The Doing Strategy®? The Learning Strategy®? Combination? Both? Neither?
_____
_____
_____
_____

○ Think about what went well and what did not go well in the past. What strategies were you using in those situations? What was in your A Circle?
_____
_____
_____
_____

○ Where do you see yourself in 3 years? You can always change your mind, but think big, think boldly, just explore in lots of different areas of your life.
_____
_____
_____
_____

O Think about your past — what has been in the way of you being successful? Purge it, write without judgment, move through these things so beyond it you can see the opportunity. Write about the opportunity beyond the struggle.

O Now look at all these things that were in your way. Turn each one around and decide how you can be grateful for each.

TUESDAY DAILY JOURNALING   DATE _____

JOURNALING PROMPTS

- Pick your intentional word or phrase of the day.
  _____

- How did yesterday's intentional word of the day or phrase support you?
  _____
  _____
  _____

- How did you use the Doing Strategy®, Learning Strategy®, and A-Circle®?
  _____
  _____
  _____
  _____
  _____

- Name a couple of examples where now looking back, you were able to use the strategies to move toward your goal.
  _____
  _____
  _____
  _____
  _____

- What went well yesterday?
  _____
  _____
  _____

- Think about the strategy you were using to do that well? What was it?
  _____
  _____
  _____

- Where can you practice that same strategy moving forward?

- How can this strategy help you achieve your goal in the next 3 months?

- Lets talk about difficult situations. Write down examples of situations for you where you felt victimized, or you felt bad, maybe something or someone that made you feel terrible. Just write things down and get them out.

- In these situations what was in your A Circle?

- Now looking back, think about how you could have supported yourself, or taken care of yourself better. What could you have had in your A Circle to support you?

- What inspired you today?

WEDNESDAY DAILY JOURNALING   DATE _____

JOURNALING PROMPTS

- Pick your intentional word or phrase of the day.
  _____

- How did yesterday's intentional word of the day or phrase support you and shift your mentality?
  _____
  _____

- This week, can you think of examples where you were able to just "do" your skills/game/sport? The Doing Strategy®?
  _____
  _____
  _____

- When you think of the Learning Strategy®, do you like to see your way through your skills/plays/sport? Feel your way through? Talk your way through? Think your way through? Or a combination? Think of a skill/play/situation where you can practice it. What do you want to be focusing on?
  _____
  _____
  _____

- Can you practice using this strategy moving forward? Where?
  _____
  _____
  _____

- Think of a time in your past where you felt confident. Explain your experience.
  _____
  _____
  _____

- When you think back to that experience, go back INTO that experience. Now, as you step out of it, how were you confident? Was it something you felt, something you saw, something you said to yourself, something you heard, or a combination?

  _____
  _____
  _____

- Can you practice this strategy moving forward to be more confident?

  _____
  _____

- Think about experiences for you in the past where you were confident. What was in your A Circle?

  _____
  _____

- Remember, your goal is seeking you as much as you are seeking it. Name 3 things that you have been working on this week that are moving you toward your goal.

  _____
  _____
  _____

- Think about your situation. What are some great things about your situation (coaches, team, parents, club/school) that can support you to achieve your goals?

  _____
  _____
  _____
  _____

- Now as you are more aware of these resources, how can you use them more to support you?

  _____
  _____
  _____

THURSDAY DAILY JOURNALING   DATE _____

JOURNALING PROMPTS

- Pick your intentional word or phrase of the day. Pick something that keeps you aligned with your "goal self." _____

- Remember that you have a "present self" and a "goal self." Practice stepping out of your "present self" and stepping into your "goal self" more often. Where have you done that? Where can you do it more?

  _____
  _____
  _____
  _____

- Do you have situations where your A Circle gets crowded with negative thoughts or negative energy or negative people? Are you having trouble kicking them out? If you are struggling with negative things in your A Circle, remember that they were once there for a good reason. So think of a situation where something negative would not leave your A Circle. Now ask yourself what that good reason was that it was there in the first place.

  _____
  _____
  _____
  _____

- An example: if you have fear/anxiety/worry in your A Circle, it is only there to help you pay attention, think about what you want to be doing, or reminding you to focus on what you are doing physically. Practice thanking that energy (yes thanking) so you can use it to your advantage. Think of old situations and practice doing this. What could you have done to support you better in the past?

  _____
  _____
  _____
  _____

- Think of some goals outside of your sport that you want to achieve. What are they?

- Can you see how these tools and strategies can support you to achieve them? How?

- Can you see how you can use these tools and strategies to support your team? You do not have to do anything extra other than recognize where your teammates are more connected mentally. Acknowledge that for them —that acknowledgment will come back to support you as well. Where could you have done this in the past?

- You can only see in others what you have in yourself. If it is negative, consider working on your own reflection. What are you reflecting out into the world? Where are you not showing up for yourself? How do you want to change that?

FRIDAY DAILY JOURNALING   DATE _____

JOURNALING PROMPTS

○ Pick your intentional word or phrase of the day. Think about your week. What can you focus on today that will support your entire week?

   _____

○ Can you think of situations this week where you were more in your own A Circle?

   _____
   _____
   _____
   _____

○ How was that helpful for you?

   _____
   _____
   _____
   _____

○ When you think about your A Circle, can you see how your managing of it can be helpful for your goals? What did you learn this week about how you are able to manage your A Circle?

   _____
   _____
   _____
   _____

○ Think of situations in the past that did not go well. An injury? Maybe you broke down under pressure, or you were worried about what people were thinking of you. Write them down.

   _____
   _____
   _____
   _____

- Looking back, do you see that if you would have known these tools and strategies, they would have been helpful? Remember, you did the best you could with what you knew at the time. What strategies could you have used? What could you have had in your A Circle?

  _____
  _____
  _____
  _____
  _____
  _____

- This week, when you look back, name 3 reasons for your success.

  _____
  _____
  _____
  _____

- What do you do well? How do you do it well? Remember: nobody does your skills/sport/game better than you —be confident in that.

  _____
  _____
  _____
  _____
  _____
  _____

- Step back and practice joy. Where do you have the most joy in your life? Do more of that.

  _____
  _____
  _____
  _____
  _____
  _____

I AM SO PROUD OF YOU!

SATURDAY DAILY JOURNALING   DATE _____

CELEBRATION DAY!

- Think of 5 situations where you were successful. Write them down.

_____
_____
_____
_____
_____
_____

- Think of 5 things that you accomplished this week. Write them down.

_____
_____
_____
_____
_____
_____

- Where did you build strength this week mentally? Physically?

_____
_____
_____
_____
_____
_____

- What did you learn from this week that can support you to achieve your goals?

_____
_____
_____
_____
_____
_____

- What went well? What didn't go well? And what can you learn from both?

- Remember that you are not equal to the result. When you accomplish a goal, it is fantastic —*but you are not equal to it*. Learn from it so you can use that experience and same strategy to build success. Where this week can you use this?

- Also, you are not equal to the mistake, or what did not go well. Separate yourself from those situations so that you can also learn from them. Can you think of any situation this week where you can practice this? Are you hard on yourself? Do you have high expectations of yourself? That's okay, but neither of those things belong in your A Circle when you are doing your sport. Did you have situations this week where this got in your way?

SUNDAY! DAILY JOURNALING   DATE _____

DREAM DAY!

O Give yourself permission to dream. We need to practice dreaming. It's not a bad thing to desire, or to want things in your life! Putting your best self into your life, sharing your gift to the world, being more of you, is your responsibility and your job. Dreaming only inspires more of you in that way. As you practice putting more of you into your life, you can share that with others; that is inspiring. Where this week were you more of you?

_____
_____
_____
_____
_____

O Regarding your answer above, were people receptive to it or a little bit threatened?

_____
_____
_____

Remember this: I can only see in you what I have in myself. So, if I don't see you in all your brightness, it's not because something is wrong with you. It is my lack that is the issue. Do not let someone else's inability to see your light dim it. Practice being your light. Practice seeing other's light as well.

O Practice these 5 mindset rules:
1. Set big, bold, tremendous goals.
2. Be grateful for everything you have today, and everything you don't have yet.
3. Be 100% accountable for your life. It doesn't mean that everything is your fault, but taking 100% responsibility for it moves you forward with strength.
4. Be thankful – for everything that went well and for everything that didn't go well.
5. Act, speak, think, and perform from the perspective of your Goal Beyond The Goal®.

Practice these mindset rules EVERY day.

MONDAY DAILY JOURNALING   DATE _____

MENTAL MINDSET FOR THE WEEK

Creating more success in your life gives you the ability to support others better. You can only give to others what you have inside. How are you using your success to support the people around you?

JOURNALING PROMPTS

○ Pick your intentional word or phrase of the day.

_____

○ Think about the past, what strategies did you use? The Doing Strategy®? The Learning Strategy®? Combination? Both? Neither?

_____
_____
_____
_____
_____

○ Think about what went well and what did not go well in the past. What strategies were you using in those situations? What was in your A Circle?

_____
_____
_____
_____

○ Where do you see yourself in 3 years? You can always change your mind, but think big, think boldly, just explore in lots of different areas of your life.

_____
_____
_____

- Think about your past — what has been in the way of you being successful? Purge it, write without judgment, move through these things so beyond it you can see the opportunity. Write about the opportunity beyond the struggle.

- Now look at all these things that were in your way. Turn each one around and decide how you can be grateful for each.

TUESDAY DAILY JOURNALING   DATE _____

JOURNALING PROMPTS

○ Pick your intentional word or phrase of the day.
_____

○ How did yesterday's intentional word of the day or phrase support you?
_____
_____
_____

○ How did you use the Doing Strategy®, Learning Strategy®, and A-Circle®?
_____
_____
_____
_____
_____

○ Name a couple of examples where now looking back, you were able to use the strategies to move toward your goal.
_____
_____
_____
_____
_____

○ What went well yesterday?
_____
_____

○ Think about the strategy you were using to do that well? What was it?
_____
_____
_____

- Where can you practice that same strategy moving forward?

- How can this strategy help you achieve your goal in the next 3 months?

- Lets talk about difficult situations. Write down examples of situations for you where you felt victimized, or you felt bad, maybe something or someone that made you feel terrible. Just write things down and get them out.

- In these situations what was in your A Circle?

- Now looking back, think about how you could have supported yourself, or taken care of yourself better. What could you have had in your A Circle to support you?

- What inspired you today?

WEDNESDAY DAILY JOURNALING   DATE _____

JOURNALING PROMPTS

○ Pick your intentional word or phrase of the day.
_____

○ How did yesterday's intentional word of the day or phrase support you and shift your mentality?
_____
_____

○ This week, can you think of examples where you were able to just "do" your skills/game/sport? The Doing Strategy®?
_____
_____
_____

○ When you think of the Learning Strategy®, do you like to see your way through your skills/plays/sport? Feel your way through? Talk your way through? Think your way through? Or a combination? Think of a skill/play/situation where you can practice it. What do you want to be focusing on?
_____
_____
_____

○ Can you practice using this strategy moving forward? Where?
_____
_____
_____

○ Think of a time in your past where you felt confident. Explain your experience.
_____
_____
_____

- When you think back to that experience, go back INTO that experience. Now, as you step out of it, how were you confident? Was it something you felt, something you saw, something you said to yourself, something you heard, or a combination?

  _____
  _____
  _____
  _____

- Can you practice this strategy moving forward to be more confident?

  _____
  _____

- Think about experiences for you in the past where you were confident. What was in your A Circle?

  _____
  _____

- Remember, your goal is seeking you as much as you are seeking it. Name 3 things that you have been working on this week that are moving you toward your goal.

  _____
  _____
  _____

- Think about your situation. What are some great things about your situation (coaches, team, parents, club/school) that can support you to achieve your goals?

  _____
  _____
  _____
  _____

- Now as you are more aware of these resources, how can you use them more to support you?

  _____
  _____
  _____

THURSDAY DAILY JOURNALING   DATE _____

JOURNALING PROMPTS

○ Pick your intentional word or phrase of the day. Pick something that keeps you aligned with your "goal self." _____

○ Remember that you have a "present self" and a "goal self." Practice stepping out of your "present self" and stepping into your "goal self" more often. Where have you done that? Where can you do it more?

_____
_____
_____
_____

○ Do you have situations where your A Circle gets crowded with negative thoughts or negative energy or negative people? Are you having trouble kicking them out? If you are struggling with negative things in your A Circle, remember that they were once there for a good reason. So think of a situation where something negative would not leave your A Circle. Now ask yourself what that good reason was that it was there in the first place.

_____
_____
_____
_____

○ An example: if you have fear/anxiety/worry in your A Circle, it is only there to help you pay attention, think about what you want to be doing, or reminding you to focus on what you are doing physically. Practice thanking that energy (yes thanking) so you can use it to your advantage. Think of old situations and practice doing this. What could you have done to support you better in the past?

_____
_____
_____
_____

- Think of some goals outside of your sport that you want to achieve. What are they?

- Can you see how these tools and strategies can support you to achieve them? How?

- Can you see how you can use these tools and strategies to support your team? You do not have to do anything extra other than recognize where your teammates are more connected mentally. Acknowledge that for them —that acknowledgment will come back to support you as well. Where could you have done this in the past?

- You can only see in others what you have in yourself. If it is negative, consider working on your own reflection. What are you reflecting out into the world? Where are you not showing up for yourself? How do you want to change that?

FRIDAY DAILY JOURNALING   DATE _____

JOURNALING PROMPTS

- Pick your intentional word or phrase of the day. Think about your week. What can you focus on today that will support your entire week?
  _____

- Can you think of situations this week where you were more in your own A Circle?
  _____
  _____
  _____
  _____

- How was that helpful for you?
  _____
  _____
  _____
  _____

- When you think about your A Circle, can you see how your managing of it can be helpful for your goals? What did you learn this week about how you are able to manage your A Circle?
  _____
  _____
  _____
  _____

- Think of situations in the past that did not go well. An injury? Maybe you broke down under pressure, or you were worried about what people were thinking of you. Write them down.
  _____
  _____
  _____
  _____

- Looking back, do you see that if you would have known these tools and strategies, they would have been helpful? Remember, you did the best you could with what you knew at the time. What strategies could you have used? What could you have had in your A Circle?

  _____
  _____
  _____
  _____
  _____
  _____

- This week, when you look back, name 3 reasons for your success.

  _____
  _____
  _____
  _____

- What do you do well? How do you do it well? Remember: nobody does your skills/sport/game better than you —be confident in that.

  _____
  _____
  _____
  _____
  _____
  _____

- Step back and practice joy. Where do you have the most joy in your life? Do more of that.

  _____
  _____
  _____
  _____
  _____
  _____

I AM SO PROUD OF YOU!

SATURDAY DAILY JOURNALING   DATE _____

CELEBRATION DAY!

O Think of 5 situations where you were successful. Write them down.

_____
_____
_____
_____
_____
_____

O Think of 5 things that you accomplished this week. Write them down.

_____
_____
_____
_____
_____
_____

O Where did you build strength this week mentally? Physically?

_____
_____
_____
_____
_____
_____

O What did you learn from this week that can support you to achieve your goals?

_____
_____
_____
_____
_____
_____

- What went well? What didn't go well? And what can you learn from both?

  _____
  _____
  _____
  _____
  _____
  _____

- Remember that you are not equal to the result. When you accomplish a goal, it is fantastic —*but you are not equal to it*. Learn from it so you can use that experience and same strategy to build success. Where this week can you use this?

  _____
  _____
  _____
  _____
  _____
  _____
  _____

- Also, you are not equal to the mistake, or what did not go well. Separate yourself from those situations so that you can also learn from them. Can you think of any situation this week where you can practice this? Are you hard on yourself? Do you have high expectations of yourself? That's okay, but neither of those things belong in your A Circle when you are doing your sport. Did you have situations this week where this got in your way?

  _____
  _____
  _____
  _____
  _____
  _____
  _____

SUNDAY! DAILY JOURNALING   DATE _____

DREAM DAY!

O Give yourself permission to dream. We need to practice dreaming. It's not a bad thing to desire, or to want things in your life! Putting your best self into your life, sharing your gift to the world, being more of you, is your responsibility and your job. Dreaming only inspires more of you in that way. As you practice putting more of you into your life, you can share that with others; that is inspiring. Where this week were you more of you?

_____
_____
_____
_____

O Regarding your answer above, were people receptive to it or a little bit threatened?

_____
_____

   Remember this: I can only see in you what I have in myself. So, if I don't see you in all your brightness, it's not because something is wrong with you. It is my lack that is the issue. Do not let someone else's inability to see your light dim it. Practice being your light. Practice seeing other's light as well.

O Practice these 5 mindset rules:
   1. Set big, bold, tremendous goals.
   2. Be grateful for everything you have today, and everything you don't have yet.
   3. Be 100% accountable for your life. It doesn't mean that everything is your fault, but taking 100% responsibility for it moves you forward with strength.
   4. Be thankful – for everything that went well and for everything that didn't go well.
   5. Act, speak, think, and perform from the perspective of your Goal Beyond The Goal®.

   Practice these mindset rules EVERY day.

MONDAY DAILY JOURNALING   DATE _____

MENTAL MINDSET FOR THE WEEK

As we come up on the first month's end, go to the Facebook group Mental Strength Coaching Journal For Athletes and share your experiences with me. I'd love to hear!

JOURNALING PROMPTS

○ Pick your intentional word or phrase of the day.

_____

○ Think about the past, what strategies did you use? The Doing Strategy®? The Learning Strategy®? Combination? Both? Neither?

_____
_____
_____
_____

○ Think about what went well and what did not go well in the past. What strategies were you using in those situations? What was in your A Circle?

_____
_____
_____
_____

○ Where do you see yourself in 3 years? You can always change your mind, but think big, think boldly, just explore in lots of different areas of your life.

_____
_____
_____
_____
_____

- Think about your past — what has been in the way of you being successful? Purge it, write without judgment, move through these things so beyond it you can see the opportunity. Write about the opportunity beyond the struggle.

- Now look at all these things that were in your way. Turn each one around and decide how you can be grateful for each.

TUESDAY DAILY JOURNALING   DATE _____

JOURNALING PROMPTS

- Pick your intentional word or phrase of the day.

- How did yesterday's intentional word of the day or phrase support you?

- How did you use the Doing Strategy®, Learning Strategy®, and A-Circle®?

- Name a couple of examples where now looking back, you were able to use the strategies to move toward your goal.

- What went well yesterday?

- Think about the strategy you were using to do that well? What was it?

- Where can you practice that same strategy moving forward?

- How can this strategy help you achieve your goal in the next 3 months?

- Lets talk about difficult situations. Write down examples of situations for you where you felt victimized, or you felt bad, maybe something or someone that made you feel terrible. Just write things down and get them out.

- In these situations what was in your A Circle?

- Now looking back, think about how you could have supported yourself, or taken care of yourself better. What could you have had in your A Circle to support you?

- What inspired you today?

WEDNESDAY DAILY JOURNALING   DATE _____

JOURNALING PROMPTS

○ Pick your intentional word or phrase of the day.
_____

○ How did yesterday's intentional word of the day or phrase support you and shift your mentality?
_____
_____

○ This week, can you think of examples where you were able to just "do" your skills/game/sport? The Doing Strategy®?
_____
_____
_____

○ When you think of the Learning Strategy®, do you like to see your way through your skills/plays/sport? Feel your way through? Talk your way through? Think your way through? Or a combination? Think of a skill/play/situation where you can practice it. What do you want to be focusing on?
_____
_____
_____

○ Can you practice using this strategy moving forward? Where?
_____
_____
_____

○ Think of a time in your past where you felt confident. Explain your experience.
_____
_____
_____

- When you think back to that experience, go back INTO that experience. Now, as you step out of it, how were you confident? Was it something you felt, something you saw, something you said to yourself, something you heard, or a combination?

  _____
  _____
  _____

- Can you practice this strategy moving forward to be more confident?

  _____
  _____

- Think about experiences for you in the past where you were confident. What was in your A Circle?

  _____
  _____

- Remember, your goal is seeking you as much as you are seeking it. Name 3 things that you have been working on this week that are moving you toward your goal.

  _____
  _____
  _____

- Think about your situation. What are some great things about your situation (coaches, team, parents, club/school) that can support you to achieve your goals?

  _____
  _____
  _____
  _____

- Now as you are more aware of these resources, how can you use them more to support you?

  _____
  _____
  _____

THURSDAY DAILY JOURNALING   DATE _____

JOURNALING PROMPTS

- Pick your intentional word or phrase of the day. Pick something that keeps you aligned with your "goal self." _____

- Remember that you have a "present self" and a "goal self." Practice stepping out of your "present self" and stepping into your "goal self" more often. Where have you done that? Where can you do it more?

  _____
  _____
  _____
  _____

- Do you have situations where your A Circle gets crowded with negative thoughts or negative energy or negative people? Are you having trouble kicking them out? If you are struggling with negative things in your A Circle, remember that they were once there for a good reason. So think of a situation where something negative would not leave your A Circle. Now ask yourself what that good reason was that it was there in the first place.

  _____
  _____
  _____
  _____

- An example: if you have fear/anxiety/worry in your A Circle, it is only there to help you pay attention, think about what you want to be doing, or reminding you to focus on what you are doing physically. Practice thanking that energy (yes thanking) so you can use it to your advantage. Think of old situations and practice doing this. What could you have done to support you better in the past?

  _____
  _____
  _____
  _____

- Think of some goals outside of your sport that you want to achieve. What are they?

- Can you see how these tools and strategies can support you to achieve them? How?

- Can you see how you can use these tools and strategies to support your team? You do not have to do anything extra other than recognize where your teammates are more connected mentally. Acknowledge that for them —that acknowledgment will come back to support you as well. Where could you have done this in the past?

- You can only see in others what you have in yourself. If it is negative, consider working on your own reflection. What are you reflecting out into the world? Where are you not showing up for yourself? How do you want to change that?

FRIDAY DAILY JOURNALING   DATE _____

JOURNALING PROMPTS

- Pick your intentional word or phrase of the day. Think about your week. What can you focus on today that will support your entire week?

  _____

- Can you think of situations this week where you were more in your own A Circle?

  _____
  _____
  _____
  _____

- How was that helpful for you?

  _____
  _____
  _____
  _____

- When you think about your A Circle, can you see how your managing of it can be helpful for your goals? What did you learn this week about how you are able to manage your A Circle?

  _____
  _____
  _____
  _____

- Think of situations in the past that did not go well. An injury? Maybe you broke down under pressure, or you were worried about what people were thinking of you. Write them down.

  _____
  _____
  _____
  _____

- Looking back, do you see that if you would have known these tools and strategies, they would have been helpful? Remember, you did the best you could with what you knew at the time. What strategies could you have used? What could you have had in your A Circle?

- This week, when you look back, name 3 reasons for your success.

- What do you do well? How do you do it well? Remember: nobody does your skills/sport/game better than you —be confident in that.

- Step back and practice joy. Where do you have the most joy in your life? Do more of that.

I AM SO PROUD OF YOU!

SATURDAY DAILY JOURNALING   DATE _____

CELEBRATION DAY!

- Think of 5 situations where you were successful. Write them down.

  _____
  _____
  _____
  _____
  _____
  _____

- Think of 5 things that you accomplished this week. Write them down.

  _____
  _____
  _____
  _____
  _____
  _____

- Where did you build strength this week mentally? Physically?

  _____
  _____
  _____
  _____
  _____
  _____

- What did you learn from this week that can support you to achieve your goals?

  _____
  _____
  _____
  _____
  _____
  _____

- What went well? What didn't go well? And what can you learn from both?

- Remember that you are not equal to the result. When you accomplish a goal, it is fantastic —*but you are not equal to it*. Learn from it so you can use that experience and same strategy to build success. Where this week can you use this?

- Also, you are not equal to the mistake, or what did not go well. Separate yourself from those situations so that you can also learn from them. Can you think of any situation this week where you can practice this? Are you hard on yourself? Do you have high expectations of yourself? That's okay, but neither of those things belong in your A Circle when you are doing your sport. Did you have situations this week where this got in your way?

SUNDAY! DAILY JOURNALING   DATE _____

DREAM DAY!

- Give yourself permission to dream. We need to practice dreaming. It's not a bad thing to desire, or to want things in your life! Putting your best self into your life, sharing your gift to the world, being more of you, is your responsibility and your job. Dreaming only inspires more of you in that way. As you practice putting more of you into your life, you can share that with others; that is inspiring. Where this week were you more of you?

  _____
  _____
  _____
  _____

- Regarding your answer above, were people receptive to it or a little bit threatened?

  _____
  _____

  > Remember this: I can only see in you what I have in myself. So, if I don't see you in all your brightness, it's not because something is wrong with you. It is my lack that is the issue. Do not let someone else's inability to see your light dim it. Practice being your light. Practice seeing other's light as well.

- Practice these 5 mindset rules:
  1. Set big, bold, tremendous goals.
  2. Be grateful for everything you have today, and everything you don't have yet.
  3. Be 100% accountable for your life. It doesn't mean that everything is your fault, but taking 100% responsibility for it moves you forward with strength.
  4. Be thankful – for everything that went well and for everything that didn't go well.
  5. Act, speak, think, and perform from the perspective of your Goal Beyond The Goal®.

  Practice these mindset rules EVERY day.

MONDAY DAILY JOURNALING   DATE _____

MENTAL MINDSET FOR THE WEEK

What do you need to be physically stronger and better? Do you need to focus on getting energy through your body? Breathing deep, foam rolling, or better cardio training can help. Remember that oxygen is energy.

JOURNALING PROMPTS

○ Pick your intentional word or phrase of the day.

_____

○ Think about the past, what strategies did you use? The Doing Strategy®? The Learning Strategy®? Combination? Both? Neither?

_____
_____
_____
_____

○ Think about what went well and what did not go well in the past. What strategies were you using in those situations? What was in your A Circle?

_____
_____
_____
_____

○ Where do you see yourself in 3 years? You can always change your mind, but think big, think boldly, just explore in lots of different areas of your life.

_____
_____
_____
_____

- Think about your past — what has been in the way of you being successful? Purge it, write without judgment, move through these things so beyond it you can see the opportunity. Write about the opportunity beyond the struggle.

- Now look at all these things that were in your way. Turn each one around and decide how you can be grateful for each.

TUESDAY DAILY JOURNALING   DATE _____

JOURNALING PROMPTS

O Pick your intentional word or phrase of the day.
_____

O How did yesterday's intentional word of the day or phrase support you?
_____
_____
_____

O How did you use the Doing Strategy®, Learning Strategy®, and A-Circle®?
_____
_____
_____
_____
_____

O Name a couple of examples where now looking back, you were able to use the strategies to move toward your goal.
_____
_____
_____
_____
_____

O What went well yesterday?
_____
_____
_____

O Think about the strategy you were using to do that well? What was it?
_____
_____
_____

- Where can you practice that same strategy moving forward?

_____
_____
_____

- How can this strategy help you achieve your goal in the next 3 months?

_____
_____
_____

- Lets talk about difficult situations. Write down examples of situations for you where you felt victimized, or you felt bad, maybe something or someone that made you feel terrible. Just write things down and get them out.

_____
_____
_____

- In these situations what was in your A Circle?

_____
_____

- Now looking back, think about how you could have supported yourself, or taken care of yourself better. What could you have had in your A Circle to support you?

_____
_____
_____
_____

- What inspired you today?

_____
_____
_____
_____

WEDNESDAY DAILY JOURNALING   DATE _____

JOURNALING PROMPTS

- Pick your intentional word or phrase of the day.
  _____

- How did yesterday's intentional word of the day or phrase support you and shift your mentality?
  _____
  _____

- This week, can you think of examples where you were able to just "do" your skills/game/sport? The Doing Strategy®?
  _____
  _____
  _____

- When you think of the Learning Strategy®, do you like to see your way through your skills/plays/sport? Feel your way through? Talk your way through? Think your way through? Or a combination? Think of a skill/play/situation where you can practice it. What do you want to be focusing on?
  _____
  _____
  _____

- Can you practice using this strategy moving forward? Where?
  _____
  _____
  _____

- Think of a time in your past where you felt confident. Explain your experience.
  _____
  _____
  _____

- When you think back to that experience, go back INTO that experience. Now, as you step out of it, how were you confident? Was it something you felt, something you saw, something you said to yourself, something you heard, or a combination?

  _____
  _____
  _____

- Can you practice this strategy moving forward to be more confident?

  _____
  _____

- Think about experiences for you in the past where you were confident. What was in your A Circle?

  _____
  _____

- Remember, your goal is seeking you as much as you are seeking it. Name 3 things that you have been working on this week that are moving you toward your goal.

  _____
  _____
  _____

- Think about your situation. What are some great things about your situation (coaches, team, parents, club/school) that can support you to achieve your goals?

  _____
  _____
  _____
  _____

- Now as you are more aware of these resources, how can you use them more to support you?

  _____
  _____
  _____

THURSDAY DAILY JOURNALING   DATE _____

JOURNALING PROMPTS

- Pick your intentional word or phrase of the day. Pick something that keeps you aligned with your "goal self." _____

- Remember that you have a "present self" and a "goal self." Practice stepping out of your "present self" and stepping into your "goal self" more often. Where have you done that? Where can you do it more?

  _____
  _____
  _____
  _____

- Do you have situations where your A Circle gets crowded with negative thoughts or negative energy or negative people? Are you having trouble kicking them out? If you are struggling with negative things in your A Circle, remember that they were once there for a good reason. So think of a situation where something negative would not leave your A Circle. Now ask yourself what that good reason was that it was there in the first place.

  _____
  _____
  _____
  _____

- An example: if you have fear/anxiety/worry in your A Circle, it is only there to help you pay attention, think about what you want to be doing, or reminding you to focus on what you are doing physically. Practice thanking that energy (yes thanking) so you can use it to your advantage. Think of old situations and practice doing this. What could you have done to support you better in the past?

  _____
  _____
  _____
  _____

- Think of some goals outside of your sport that you want to achieve. What are they?

  _____
  _____
  _____
  _____
  _____

- Can you see how these tools and strategies can support you to achieve them? How?

  _____
  _____
  _____
  _____
  _____

- Can you see how you can use these tools and strategies to support your team? You do not have to do anything extra other than recognize where your teammates are more connected mentally. Acknowledge that for them —that acknowledgment will come back to support you as well. Where could you have done this in the past?

  _____
  _____
  _____
  _____
  _____

- You can only see in others what you have in yourself. If it is negative, consider working on your own reflection. What are you reflecting out into the world? Where are you not showing up for yourself? How do you want to change that?

  _____
  _____
  _____
  _____
  _____

FRIDAY DAILY JOURNALING   DATE _____

JOURNALING PROMPTS

- Pick your intentional word or phrase of the day. Think about your week. What can you focus on today that will support your entire week?
  _____

- Can you think of situations this week where you were more in your own A Circle?
  _____
  _____
  _____
  _____

- How was that helpful for you?
  _____
  _____
  _____
  _____

- When you think about your A Circle, can you see how your managing of it can be helpful for your goals? What did you learn this week about how you are able to manage your A Circle?
  _____
  _____
  _____
  _____

- Think of situations in the past that did not go well. An injury? Maybe you broke down under pressure, or you were worried about what people were thinking of you. Write them down.
  _____
  _____
  _____
  _____

- Looking back, do you see that if you would have known these tools and strategies, they would have been helpful? Remember, you did the best you could with what you knew at the time. What strategies could you have used? What could you have had in your A Circle?

- This week, when you look back, name 3 reasons for your success.

- What do you do well? How do you do it well? Remember: nobody does your skills/sport/game better than you —be confident in that.

- Step back and practice joy. Where do you have the most joy in your life? Do more of that.

I AM SO PROUD OF YOU!

SATURDAY DAILY JOURNALING   DATE _____

CELEBRATION DAY!

O Think of 5 situations where you were successful. Write them down.

_____
_____
_____
_____
_____
_____

O Think of 5 things that you accomplished this week. Write them down.

_____
_____
_____
_____
_____
_____

O Where did you build strength this week mentally? Physically?

_____
_____
_____
_____
_____
_____

O What did you learn from this week that can support you to achieve your goals?

_____
_____
_____
_____
_____
_____

- What went well? What didn't go well? And what can you learn from both?

- Remember that you are not equal to the result. When you accomplish a goal, it is fantastic —*but you are not equal to it.* Learn from it so you can use that experience and same strategy to build success. Where this week can you use this?

- Also, you are not equal to the mistake, or what did not go well. Separate yourself from those situations so that you can also learn from them. Can you think of any situation this week where you can practice this? Are you hard on yourself? Do you have high expectations of yourself? That's okay, but neither of those things belong in your A Circle when you are doing your sport. Did you have situations this week where this got in your way?

SUNDAY! DAILY JOURNALING   DATE _____

DREAM DAY!

- Give yourself permission to dream. We need to practice dreaming. It's not a bad thing to desire, or to want things in your life! Putting your best self into your life, sharing your gift to the world, being more of you, is your responsibility and your job. Dreaming only inspires more of you in that way. As you practice putting more of you into your life, you can share that with others; that is inspiring. Where this week were you more of you?

  _____
  _____
  _____
  _____

- Regarding your answer above, were people receptive to it or a little bit threatened?

  _____
  _____

  Remember this: I can only see in you what I have in myself. So, if I don't see you in all your brightness, it's not because something is wrong with you. It is my lack that is the issue. Do not let someone else's inability to see your light dim it. Practice being your light. Practice seeing other's light as well.

- Practice these 5 mindset rules:
  1. Set big, bold, tremendous goals.
  2. Be grateful for everything you have today, and everything you don't have yet.
  3. Be 100% accountable for your life. It doesn't mean that everything is your fault, but taking 100% responsibility for it moves you forward with strength.
  4. Be thankful – for everything that went well and for everything that didn't go well.
  5. Act, speak, think, and perform from the perspective of your Goal Beyond The Goal®.

  Practice these mindset rules EVERY day.

MONTH _____ 20 _____

MONDAY	TUESDAY	WEDNESDAY	THURSDAY

NOBODY DOES *YOU* IN YOUR SPORT BETTER THAN YOU.
BE CONFIDENT IN THAT.

© Stacey Herman Goodrich

FRIDAY   SATURDAY   SUNDAY

MONDAY DAILY JOURNALING   DATE _____

MENTAL MINDSET FOR THE WEEK

Think about what continues to show up in your A Circle. Is it positive or negative? Ask yourself why you need it, and as you let it go, replace it with what you want *now*. Use it to your advantage.

JOURNALING PROMPTS

- Pick your intentional word or phrase of the day.
  _____

- Think about the past, what strategies did you use? The Doing Strategy®? The Learning Strategy®? Combination? Both? Neither?
  _____
  _____
  _____
  _____
  _____

- Think about what went well and what did not go well in the past. What strategies were you using in those situations? What was in your A Circle?
  _____
  _____
  _____
  _____
  _____

- Where do you see yourself in 3 years? You can always change your mind, but think big, think boldly, just explore in lots of different areas of your life.
  _____
  _____
  _____

- Think about your past — what has been in the way of you being successful? Purge it, write without judgment, move through these things so beyond it you can see the opportunity. Write about the opportunity beyond the struggle.

- Now look at all these things that were in your way. Turn each one around and decide how you can be grateful for each.

TUESDAY DAILY JOURNALING   DATE _____

JOURNALING PROMPTS

- Pick your intentional word or phrase of the day.
  _____

- How did yesterday's intentional word of the day or phrase support you?
  _____
  _____
  _____

- How did you use the Doing Strategy®, Learning Strategy®, and A-Circle®?
  _____
  _____
  _____
  _____

- Name a couple of examples where now looking back, you were able to use the strategies to move toward your goal.
  _____
  _____
  _____
  _____
  _____

- What went well yesterday?
  _____
  _____
  _____

- Think about the strategy you were using to do that well? What was it?
  _____
  _____
  _____

- Where can you practice that same strategy moving forward?
  ___
  ___
  ___

- How can this strategy help you achieve your goal in the next 3 months?
  ___
  ___
  ___

- Lets talk about difficult situations. Write down examples of situations for you where you felt victimized, or you felt bad, maybe something or someone that made you feel terrible. Just write things down and get them out.
  ___
  ___
  ___

- In these situations what was in your A Circle?
  ___
  ___

- Now looking back, think about how you could have supported yourself, or taken care of yourself better. What could you have had in your A Circle to support you?
  ___
  ___
  ___

- What inspired you today?
  ___
  ___
  ___

WEDNESDAY DAILY JOURNALING   DATE _____

JOURNALING PROMPTS

- Pick your intentional word or phrase of the day.
  _____

- How did yesterday's intentional word of the day or phrase support you and shift your mentality?
  _____
  _____

- This week, can you think of examples where you were able to just "do" your skills/game/sport? The Doing Strategy®?
  _____
  _____
  _____

- When you think of the Learning Strategy®, do you like to see your way through your skills/plays/sport? Feel your way through? Talk your way through? Think your way through? Or a combination? Think of a skill/play/situation where you can practice it. What do you want to be focusing on?
  _____
  _____
  _____

- Can you practice using this strategy moving forward? Where?
  _____
  _____
  _____

- Think of a time in your past where you felt confident. Explain your experience.
  _____
  _____
  _____

- When you think back to that experience, go back INTO that experience. Now, as you step out of it, how were you confident? Was it something you felt, something you saw, something you said to yourself, something you heard, or a combination?

  _____
  _____
  _____

- Can you practice this strategy moving forward to be more confident?

  _____
  _____

- Think about experiences for you in the past where you were confident. What was in your A Circle?

  _____
  _____

- Remember, your goal is seeking you as much as you are seeking it. Name 3 things that you have been working on this week that are moving you toward your goal.

  _____
  _____
  _____

- Think about your situation. What are some great things about your situation (coaches, team, parents, club/school) that can support you to achieve your goals?

  _____
  _____
  _____
  _____

- Now as you are more aware of these resources, how can you use them more to support you?

  _____
  _____
  _____

THURSDAY DAILY JOURNALING   DATE _____

JOURNALING PROMPTS

- Pick your intentional word or phrase of the day. Pick something that keeps you aligned with your "goal self." _____

- Remember that you have a "present self" and a "goal self." Practice stepping out of your "present self" and stepping into your "goal self" more often. Where have you done that? Where can you do it more?

  _____
  _____
  _____

- Do you have situations where your A Circle gets crowded with negative thoughts or negative energy or negative people? Are you having trouble kicking them out? If you are struggling with negative things in your A Circle, remember that they were once there for a good reason. So think of a situation where something negative would not leave your A Circle. Now ask yourself what that good reason was that it was there in the first place.

  _____
  _____
  _____

- An example: if you have fear/anxiety/worry in your A Circle, it is only there to help you pay attention, think about what you want to be doing, or reminding you to focus on what you are doing physically. Practice thanking that energy (yes thanking) so you can use it to your advantage. Think of old situations and practice doing this. What could you have done to support you better in the past?

  _____
  _____
  _____

- Think of some goals outside of your sport that you want to achieve. What are they?

  _____
  _____
  _____
  _____
  _____

- Can you see how these tools and strategies can support you to achieve them? How?

  _____
  _____
  _____
  _____
  _____

- Can you see how you can use these tools and strategies to support your team? You do not have to do anything extra other than recognize where your teammates are more connected mentally. Acknowledge that for them —that acknowledgment will come back to support you as well. Where could you have done this in the past?

  _____
  _____
  _____
  _____
  _____
  _____

- You can only see in others what you have in yourself. If it is negative, consider working on your own reflection. What are you reflecting out into the world? Where are you not showing up for yourself? How do you want to change that?

  _____
  _____
  _____
  _____
  _____
  _____
  _____

FRIDAY DAILY JOURNALING DATE _____

JOURNALING PROMPTS

- Pick your intentional word or phrase of the day. Think about your week. What can you focus on today that will support your entire week?

  _____

- Can you think of situations this week where you were more in your own A Circle?

  _____
  _____
  _____
  _____

- How was that helpful for you?

  _____
  _____
  _____
  _____

- When you think about your A Circle, can you see how your managing of it can be helpful for your goals? What did you learn this week about how you are able to manage your A Circle?

  _____
  _____
  _____
  _____

- Think of situations in the past that did not go well. An injury? Maybe you broke down under pressure, or you were worried about what people were thinking of you. Write them down.

  _____
  _____
  _____
  _____

- Looking back, do you see that if you would have known these tools and strategies, they would have been helpful? Remember, you did the best you could with what you knew at the time. What strategies could you have used? What could you have had in your A Circle?

  _____
  _____
  _____
  _____
  _____
  _____

- This week, when you look back, name 3 reasons for your success.

  _____
  _____
  _____
  _____

- What do you do well? How do you do it well? Remember: nobody does your skills/sport/game better than you —be confident in that.

  _____
  _____
  _____
  _____
  _____
  _____

- Step back and practice joy. Where do you have the most joy in your life? Do more of that.

  _____
  _____
  _____
  _____
  _____
  _____

I AM SO PROUD OF YOU!

SATURDAY DAILY JOURNALING   DATE _____

CELEBRATION DAY!

O Think of 5 situations where you were successful. Write them down.

_____
_____
_____
_____
_____

O Think of 5 things that you accomplished this week. Write them down.

_____
_____
_____
_____
_____

O Where did you build strength this week mentally? Physically?

_____
_____
_____
_____
_____

O What did you learn from this week that can support you to achieve your goals?

_____
_____
_____
_____
_____
_____

- What went well? What didn't go well? And what can you learn from both?

- Remember that you are not equal to the result. When you accomplish a goal, it is fantastic —*but you are not equal to it.* Learn from it so you can use that experience and same strategy to build success. Where this week can you use this?

- Also, you are not equal to the mistake, or what did not go well. Separate yourself from those situations so that you can also learn from them. Can you think of any situation this week where you can practice this? Are you hard on yourself? Do you have high expectations of yourself? That's okay, but neither of those things belong in your A Circle when you are doing your sport. Did you have situations this week where this got in your way?

SUNDAY! DAILY JOURNALING   DATE _____

DREAM DAY!

- Give yourself permission to dream. We need to practice dreaming. It's not a bad thing to desire, or to want things in your life! Putting your best self into your life, sharing your gift to the world, being more of you, is your responsibility and your job. Dreaming only inspires more of you in that way. As you practice putting more of you into your life, you can share that with others; that is inspiring. Where this week were you more of you?

  _____
  _____
  _____
  _____
  _____

- Regarding your answer above, were people receptive to it or a little bit threatened?

  _____
  _____
  _____

  Remember this: I can only see in you what I have in myself. So, if I don't see you in all your brightness, it's not because something is wrong with you. It is my lack that is the issue. Do not let someone else's inability to see your light dim it. Practice being your light. Practice seeing other's light as well.

- Practice these 5 mindset rules:
  1. Set big, bold, tremendous goals.
  2. Be grateful for everything you have today, and everything you don't have yet.
  3. Be 100% accountable for your life. It doesn't mean that everything is your fault, but taking 100% responsibility for it moves you forward with strength.
  4. Be thankful – for everything that went well and for everything that didn't go well.
  5. Act, speak, think, and perform from the perspective of your Goal Beyond The Goal®.

  Practice these mindset rules EVERY day.

MONDAY DAILY JOURNALING   DATE _____

MENTAL MINDSET FOR THE WEEK

Do you keep sabotaging yourself? Reach out to me: **stacey@so-connected.com** I offer sessions one-on-one and can help you with those old patterns.

JOURNALING PROMPTS

- Pick your intentional word or phrase of the day.
  _____

- Think about the past, what strategies did you use? The Doing Strategy®? The Learning Strategy®? Combination? Both? Neither?

- Think about what went well and what did not go well in the past. What strategies were you using in those situations? What was in your A Circle?

- Where do you see yourself in 3 years? You can always change your mind, but think big, think boldly, just explore in lots of different areas of your life.

- Think about your past — what has been in the way of you being successful? Purge it, write without judgment, move through these things so beyond it you can see the opportunity. Write about the opportunity beyond the struggle.

- Now look at all these things that were in your way. Turn each one around and decide how you can be grateful for each.

TUESDAY DAILY JOURNALING   DATE _____

JOURNALING PROMPTS

- Pick your intentional word or phrase of the day.
  _____

- How did yesterday's intentional word of the day or phrase support you?
  _____
  _____
  _____

- How did you use the Doing Strategy®, Learning Strategy®, and A-Circle®?
  _____
  _____
  _____
  _____
  _____

- Name a couple of examples where now looking back, you were able to use the strategies to move toward your goal.
  _____
  _____
  _____
  _____
  _____

- What went well yesterday?
  _____
  _____
  _____

- Think about the strategy you were using to do that well? What was it?
  _____
  _____
  _____

○ Where can you practice that same strategy moving forward?
___
___
___
___

○ How can this strategy help you achieve your goal in the next 3 months?
___
___
___
___

○ Lets talk about difficult situations. Write down examples of situations for you where you felt victimized, or you felt bad, maybe something or someone that made you feel terrible. Just write things down and get them out.
___
___
___
___

○ In these situations what was in your A Circle?
___
___

○ Now looking back, think about how you could have supported yourself, or taken care of yourself better. What could you have had in your A Circle to support you?
___
___
___
___

○ What inspired you today?
___
___
___
___

WEDNESDAY DAILY JOURNALING   DATE _____

JOURNALING PROMPTS

○ Pick your intentional word or phrase of the day.
_____

○ How did yesterday's intentional word of the day or phrase support you and shift your mentality?
_____
_____

○ This week, can you think of examples where you were able to just "do" your skills/game/sport? The Doing Strategy®?
_____
_____
_____

○ When you think of the Learning Strategy®, do you like to see your way through your skills/plays/sport? Feel your way through? Talk your way through? Think your way through? Or a combination? Think of a skill/play/situation where you can practice it. What do you want to be focusing on?
_____
_____
_____

○ Can you practice using this strategy moving forward? Where?
_____
_____
_____

○ Think of a time in your past where you felt confident. Explain your experience.
_____
_____
_____

- When you think back to that experience, go back INTO that experience. Now, as you step out of it, how were you confident? Was it something you felt, something you saw, something you said to yourself, something you heard, or a combination?

  _____
  _____
  _____

- Can you practice this strategy moving forward to be more confident?

  _____
  _____

- Think about experiences for you in the past where you were confident. What was in your A Circle?

  _____
  _____

- Remember, your goal is seeking you as much as you are seeking it. Name 3 things that you have been working on this week that are moving you toward your goal.

  _____
  _____

- Think about your situation. What are some great things about your situation (coaches, team, parents, club/school) that can support you to achieve your goals?

  _____
  _____
  _____
  _____

- Now as you are more aware of these resources, how can you use them more to support you?

  _____
  _____
  _____

THURSDAY DAILY JOURNALING   DATE _____

JOURNALING PROMPTS

O Pick your intentional word or phrase of the day. Pick something that keeps you aligned with your "goal self." _____

O Remember that you have a "present self" and a "goal self." Practice stepping out of your "present self" and stepping into your "goal self" more often. Where have you done that? Where can you do it more?

_____
_____
_____
_____

O Do you have situations where your A Circle gets crowded with negative thoughts or negative energy or negative people? Are you having trouble kicking them out? If you are struggling with negative things in your A Circle, remember that they were once there for a good reason. So think of a situation where something negative would not leave your A Circle. Now ask yourself what that good reason was that it was there in the first place.

_____
_____
_____
_____

O An example: if you have fear/anxiety/worry in your A Circle, it is only there to help you pay attention, think about what you want to be doing, or reminding you to focus on what you are doing physically. Practice thanking that energy (yes thanking) so you can use it to your advantage. Think of old situations and practice doing this. What could you have done to support you better in the past?

_____
_____
_____
_____

- Think of some goals outside of your sport that you want to achieve. What are they?

- Can you see how these tools and strategies can support you to achieve them? How?

- Can you see how you can use these tools and strategies to support your team? You do not have to do anything extra other than recognize where your teammates are more connected mentally. Acknowledge that for them —that acknowledgment will come back to support you as well. Where could you have done this in the past?

- You can only see in others what you have in yourself. If it is negative, consider working on your own reflection. What are you reflecting out into the world? Where are you not showing up for yourself? How do you want to change that?

FRIDAY DAILY JOURNALING   DATE _____

JOURNALING PROMPTS

- Pick your intentional word or phrase of the day. Think about your week. What can you focus on today that will support your entire week?
  _____

- Can you think of situations this week where you were more in your own A Circle?
  _____
  _____
  _____
  _____

- How was that helpful for you?
  _____
  _____
  _____
  _____

- When you think about your A Circle, can you see how your managing of it can be helpful for your goals? What did you learn this week about how you are able to manage your A Circle?
  _____
  _____
  _____
  _____

- Think of situations in the past that did not go well. An injury? Maybe you broke down under pressure, or you were worried about what people were thinking of you. Write them down.
  _____
  _____
  _____
  _____

- Looking back, do you see that if you would have known these tools and strategies, they would have been helpful? Remember, you did the best you could with what you knew at the time. What strategies could you have used? What could you have had in your A Circle?

  _____
  _____
  _____
  _____
  _____

- This week, when you look back, name 3 reasons for your success.

  _____
  _____
  _____

- What do you do well? How do you do it well? Remember: nobody does your skills/sport/game better than you —be confident in that.

  _____
  _____
  _____
  _____
  _____

- Step back and practice joy. Where do you have the most joy in your life? Do more of that.

  _____
  _____
  _____
  _____
  _____
  _____

I AM SO PROUD OF YOU!

SATURDAY DAILY JOURNALING   DATE _____

CELEBRATION DAY!

○ Think of 5 situations where you were successful. Write them down.

_____
_____
_____
_____
_____
_____

○ Think of 5 things that you accomplished this week. Write them down.

_____
_____
_____
_____
_____
_____

○ Where did you build strength this week mentally? Physically?

_____
_____
_____
_____
_____
_____

○ What did you learn from this week that can support you to achieve your goals?

_____
_____
_____
_____
_____
_____

- What went well? What didn't go well? And what can you learn from both?

- Remember that you are not equal to the result. When you accomplish a goal, it is fantastic —*but you are not equal to it.* Learn from it so you can use that experience and same strategy to build success. Where this week can you use this?

- Also, you are not equal to the mistake, or what did not go well. Separate yourself from those situations so that you can also learn from them. Can you think of any situation this week where you can practice this? Are you hard on yourself? Do you have high expectations of yourself? That's okay, but neither of those things belong in your A Circle when you are doing your sport. Did you have situations this week where this got in your way?

SUNDAY! DAILY JOURNALING   DATE _____

DREAM DAY!

- Give yourself permission to dream. We need to practice dreaming. It's not a bad thing to desire, or to want things in your life! Putting your best self into your life, sharing your gift to the world, being more of you, is your responsibility and your job. Dreaming only inspires more of you in that way. As you practice putting more of you into your life, you can share that with others; that is inspiring. Where this week were you more of you?

  _____
  _____
  _____
  _____
  _____

- Regarding your answer above, were people receptive to it or a little bit threatened?

  _____
  _____
  _____

  Remember this: I can only see in you what I have in myself. So, if I don't see you in all your brightness, it's not because something is wrong with you. It is my lack that is the issue. Do not let someone else's inability to see your light dim it. Practice being your light. Practice seeing other's light as well.

- Practice these 5 mindset rules:
  1. Set big, bold, tremendous goals.
  2. Be grateful for everything you have today, and everything you don't have yet.
  3. Be 100% accountable for your life. It doesn't mean that everything is your fault, but taking 100% responsibility for it moves you forward with strength.
  4. Be thankful – for everything that went well and for everything that didn't go well.
  5. Act, speak, think, and perform from the perspective of your Goal Beyond The Goal®.

  Practice these mindset rules EVERY day.

MONDAY DAILY JOURNALING   DATE _____

MENTAL MINDSET FOR THE WEEK

As you achieve your goals, create more! Dream big. Think outside the box. Play more.

JOURNALING PROMPTS

- Pick your intentional word or phrase of the day.
  _____

- Think about the past, what strategies did you use? The Doing Strategy®? The Learning Strategy®? Combination? Both? Neither?

- Think about what went well and what did not go well in the past. What strategies were you using in those situations? What was in your A Circle?

- Where do you see yourself in 3 years? You can always change your mind, but think big, think boldly, just explore in lots of different areas of your life.

- Think about your past — what has been in the way of you being successful? Purge it, write without judgment, move through these things so beyond it you can see the opportunity. Write about the opportunity beyond the struggle.

- Now look at all these things that were in your way. Turn each one around and decide how you can be grateful for each.

TUESDAY DAILY JOURNALING   DATE _____

JOURNALING PROMPTS

O Pick your intentional word or phrase of the day.
   _____

O How did yesterday's intentional word of the day or phrase support you?
   _____
   _____
   _____

O How did you use the Doing Strategy®, Learning Strategy®, and A-Circle®?
   _____
   _____
   _____
   _____
   _____

O Name a couple of examples where now looking back, you were able to use the strategies to move toward your goal.
   _____
   _____
   _____
   _____
   _____

O What went well yesterday?
   _____
   _____
   _____

O Think about the strategy you were using to do that well? What was it?
   _____
   _____
   _____

- Where can you practice that same strategy moving forward?
  _____
  _____
  _____

- How can this strategy help you achieve your goal in the next 3 months?
  _____
  _____
  _____

- Lets talk about difficult situations. Write down examples of situations for you where you felt victimized, or you felt bad, maybe something or someone that made you feel terrible. Just write things down and get them out.
  _____
  _____
  _____

- In these situations what was in your A Circle?
  _____
  _____

- Now looking back, think about how you could have supported yourself, or taken care of yourself better. What could you have had in your A Circle to support you?
  _____
  _____
  _____

- What inspired you today?
  _____
  _____
  _____

WEDNESDAY DAILY JOURNALING   DATE _____

JOURNALING PROMPTS

- Pick your intentional word or phrase of the day.
  _____

- How did yesterday's intentional word of the day or phrase support you and shift your mentality?
  _____
  _____

- This week, can you think of examples where you were able to just "do" your skills/game/sport? The Doing Strategy®?
  _____
  _____
  _____

- When you think of the Learning Strategy®, do you like to see your way through your skills/plays/sport? Feel your way through? Talk your way through? Think your way through? Or a combination? Think of a skill/play/situation where you can practice it. What do you want to be focusing on?
  _____
  _____
  _____

- Can you practice using this strategy moving forward? Where?
  _____
  _____
  _____

- Think of a time in your past where you felt confident. Explain your experience.
  _____
  _____
  _____

- When you think back to that experience, go back INTO that experience. Now, as you step out of it, how were you confident? Was it something you felt, something you saw, something you said to yourself, something you heard, or a combination?

  _____
  _____
  _____

- Can you practice this strategy moving forward to be more confident?

  _____
  _____

- Think about experiences for you in the past where you were confident. What was in your A Circle?

  _____
  _____

- Remember, your goal is seeking you as much as you are seeking it. Name 3 things that you have been working on this week that are moving you toward your goal.

  _____
  _____
  _____

- Think about your situation. What are some great things about your situation (coaches, team, parents, club/school) that can support you to achieve your goals?

  _____
  _____
  _____
  _____

- Now as you are more aware of these resources, how can you use them more to support you?

  _____
  _____
  _____

THURSDAY DAILY JOURNALING   DATE _____

JOURNALING PROMPTS

- Pick your intentional word or phrase of the day. Pick something that keeps you aligned with your "goal self." _____

- Remember that you have a "present self" and a "goal self." Practice stepping out of your "present self" and stepping into your "goal self" more often. Where have you done that? Where can you do it more?

  _____
  _____
  _____
  _____

- Do you have situations where your A Circle gets crowded with negative thoughts or negative energy or negative people? Are you having trouble kicking them out? If you are struggling with negative things in your A Circle, remember that they were once there for a good reason. So think of a situation where something negative would not leave your A Circle. Now ask yourself what that good reason was that it was there in the first place.

  _____
  _____
  _____
  _____

- An example: if you have fear/anxiety/worry in your A Circle, it is only there to help you pay attention, think about what you want to be doing, or reminding you to focus on what you are doing physically. Practice thanking that energy (yes thanking) so you can use it to your advantage. Think of old situations and practice doing this. What could you have done to support you better in the past?

  _____
  _____
  _____
  _____

- Think of some goals outside of your sport that you want to achieve. What are they?

- Can you see how these tools and strategies can support you to achieve them? How?

- Can you see how you can use these tools and strategies to support your team? You do not have to do anything extra other than recognize where your teammates are more connected mentally. Acknowledge that for them —that acknowledgment will come back to support you as well. Where could you have done this in the past?

- You can only see in others what you have in yourself. If it is negative, consider working on your own reflection. What are you reflecting out into the world? Where are you not showing up for yourself? How do you want to change that?

FRIDAY DAILY JOURNALING   DATE _____

JOURNALING PROMPTS

- Pick your intentional word or phrase of the day. Think about your week. What can you focus on today that will support your entire week?
  _____

- Can you think of situations this week where you were more in your own A Circle?
  _____
  _____
  _____
  _____

- How was that helpful for you?
  _____
  _____
  _____
  _____

- When you think about your A Circle, can you see how your managing of it can be helpful for your goals? What did you learn this week about how you are able to manage your A Circle?
  _____
  _____
  _____
  _____

- Think of situations in the past that did not go well. An injury? Maybe you broke down under pressure, or you were worried about what people were thinking of you. Write them down.
  _____
  _____
  _____

- Looking back, do you see that if you would have known these tools and strategies, they would have been helpful? Remember, you did the best you could with what you knew at the time. What strategies could you have used? What could you have had in your A Circle?

  _____
  _____
  _____
  _____
  _____

- This week, when you look back, name 3 reasons for your success.

  _____
  _____
  _____

- What do you do well? How do you do it well? Remember: nobody does your skills/sport/game better than you —be confident in that.

  _____
  _____
  _____
  _____
  _____
  _____

- Step back and practice joy. Where do you have the most joy in your life? Do more of that.

  _____
  _____
  _____
  _____
  _____
  _____

I AM SO PROUD OF YOU!

SATURDAY DAILY JOURNALING   DATE _____

CELEBRATION DAY!

- Think of 5 situations where you were successful. Write them down.

  _____
  _____
  _____
  _____
  _____
  _____

- Think of 5 things that you accomplished this week. Write them down.

  _____
  _____
  _____
  _____
  _____
  _____

- Where did you build strength this week mentally? Physically?

  _____
  _____
  _____
  _____
  _____
  _____

- What did you learn from this week that can support you to achieve your goals?

  _____
  _____
  _____
  _____
  _____
  _____

- What went well? What didn't go well? And what can you learn from both?

- Remember that you are not equal to the result. When you accomplish a goal, it is fantastic —*but you are not equal to it.* Learn from it so you can use that experience and same strategy to build success. Where this week can you use this?

- Also, you are not equal to the mistake, or what did not go well. Separate yourself from those situations so that you can also learn from them. Can you think of any situation this week where you can practice this? Are you hard on yourself? Do you have high expectations of yourself? That's okay, but neither of those things belong in your A Circle when you are doing your sport. Did you have situations this week where this got in your way?

SUNDAY! DAILY JOURNALING   DATE _____

DREAM DAY!

O Give yourself permission to dream. We need to practice dreaming. It's not a bad thing to desire, or to want things in your life! Putting your best self into your life, sharing your gift to the world, being more of you, is your responsibility and your job. Dreaming only inspires more of you in that way. As you practice putting more of you into your life, you can share that with others; that is inspiring. Where this week were you more of you?

_____
_____
_____
_____
_____

O Regarding your answer above, were people receptive to it or a little bit threatened?

_____
_____
_____

Remember this: I can only see in you what I have in myself. So, if I don't see you in all your brightness, it's not because something is wrong with you. It is my lack that is the issue. Do not let someone else's inability to see your light dim it. Practice being your light. Practice seeing other's light as well.

O Practice these 5 mindset rules:
1. Set big, bold, tremendous goals.
2. Be grateful for everything you have today, and everything you don't have yet.
3. Be 100% accountable for your life. It doesn't mean that everything is your fault, but taking 100% responsibility for it moves you forward with strength.
4. Be thankful – for everything that went well and for everything that didn't go well.
5. Act, speak, think, and perform from the perspective of your Goal Beyond The Goal®.

Practice these mindset rules EVERY day.

MONDAY DAILY JOURNALING   DATE _____

MENTAL MINDSET FOR THE WEEK

Do you see how these strategies are supporting you in your relationships? Remember to support yourself within your relationships, so people you're communicating with have more of you to connect with during your interactions.

JOURNALING PROMPTS

○ Pick your intentional word or phrase of the day.

_____

○ Think about the past, what strategies did you use? The Doing Strategy®? The Learning Strategy®? Combination? Both? Neither?

_____
_____
_____
_____

○ Think about what went well and what did not go well in the past. What strategies were you using in those situations? What was in your A Circle?

_____
_____
_____
_____

○ Where do you see yourself in 3 years? You can always change your mind, but think big, think boldly, just explore in lots of different areas of your life.

_____
_____
_____
_____

O Think about your past — what has been in the way of you being successful? Purge it, write without judgment, move through these things so beyond it you can see the opportunity. Write about the opportunity beyond the struggle.

O Now look at all these things that were in your way. Turn each one around and decide how you can be grateful for each.

TUESDAY DAILY JOURNALING   DATE _____

JOURNALING PROMPTS

- Pick your intentional word or phrase of the day.
  _____

- How did yesterday's intentional word of the day or phrase support you?
  _____
  _____
  _____

- How did you use the Doing Strategy®, Learning Strategy®, and A-Circle®?
  _____
  _____
  _____
  _____
  _____

- Name a couple of examples where now looking back, you were able to use the strategies to move toward your goal.
  _____
  _____
  _____
  _____
  _____

- What went well yesterday?
  _____
  _____
  _____

- Think about the strategy you were using to do that well? What was it?
  _____
  _____
  _____

- Where can you practice that same strategy moving forward?
  _____
  _____
  _____
  _____

- How can this strategy help you achieve your goal in the next 3 months?
  _____
  _____
  _____
  _____

- Lets talk about difficult situations. Write down examples of situations for you where you felt victimized, or you felt bad, maybe something or someone that made you feel terrible. Just write things down and get them out.
  _____
  _____
  _____
  _____

- In these situations what was in your A Circle?
  _____
  _____

- Now looking back, think about how you could have supported yourself, or taken care of yourself better. What could you have had in your A Circle to support you?
  _____
  _____
  _____
  _____

- What inspired you today?
  _____
  _____
  _____
  _____

WEDNESDAY DAILY JOURNALING   DATE _____

JOURNALING PROMPTS

- Pick your intentional word or phrase of the day.
  _____

- How did yesterday's intentional word of the day or phrase support you and shift your mentality?
  _____
  _____

- This week, can you think of examples where you were able to just "do" your skills/game/sport? The Doing Strategy®?
  _____
  _____
  _____

- When you think of the Learning Strategy®, do you like to see your way through your skills/plays/sport? Feel your way through? Talk your way through? Think your way through? Or a combination? Think of a skill/play/situation where you can practice it. What do you want to be focusing on?
  _____
  _____
  _____

- Can you practice using this strategy moving forward? Where?
  _____
  _____
  _____

- Think of a time in your past where you felt confident. Explain your experience.
  _____
  _____
  _____

- When you think back to that experience, go back INTO that experience. Now, as you step out of it, how were you confident? Was it something you felt, something you saw, something you said to yourself, something you heard, or a combination?

  _____
  _____
  _____
  _____

- Can you practice this strategy moving forward to be more confident?

  _____
  _____

- Think about experiences for you in the past where you were confident. What was in your A Circle?

  _____
  _____

- Remember, your goal is seeking you as much as you are seeking it. Name 3 things that you have been working on this week that are moving you toward your goal.

  _____
  _____
  _____

- Think about your situation. What are some great things about your situation (coaches, team, parents, club/school) that can support you to achieve your goals?

  _____
  _____
  _____
  _____

- Now as you are more aware of these resources, how can you use them more to support you?

  _____
  _____
  _____

THURSDAY DAILY JOURNALING   DATE _____

JOURNALING PROMPTS

- Pick your intentional word or phrase of the day. Pick something that keeps you aligned with your "goal self." _____

- Remember that you have a "present self" and a "goal self." Practice stepping out of your "present self" and stepping into your "goal self" more often. Where have you done that? Where can you do it more?

  _____
  _____
  _____
  _____

- Do you have situations where your A Circle gets crowded with negative thoughts or negative energy or negative people? Are you having trouble kicking them out? If you are struggling with negative things in your A Circle, remember that they were once there for a good reason. So think of a situation where something negative would not leave your A Circle. Now ask yourself what that good reason was that it was there in the first place.

  _____
  _____
  _____
  _____

- An example: if you have fear/anxiety/worry in your A Circle, it is only there to help you pay attention, think about what you want to be doing, or reminding you to focus on what you are doing physically. Practice thanking that energy (yes thanking) so you can use it to your advantage. Think of old situations and practice doing this. What could you have done to support you better in the past?

  _____
  _____
  _____
  _____

- Think of some goals outside of your sport that you want to achieve. What are they?

  _____
  _____
  _____
  _____
  _____

- Can you see how these tools and strategies can support you to achieve them? How?

  _____
  _____
  _____
  _____
  _____

- Can you see how you can use these tools and strategies to support your team? You do not have to do anything extra other than recognize where your teammates are more connected mentally. Acknowledge that for them —that acknowledgment will come back to support you as well. Where could you have done this in the past?

  _____
  _____
  _____
  _____
  _____
  _____

- You can only see in others what you have in yourself. If it is negative, consider working on your own reflection. What are you reflecting out into the world? Where are you not showing up for yourself? How do you want to change that?

  _____
  _____
  _____
  _____
  _____
  _____
  _____

FRIDAY DAILY JOURNALING   DATE _____

JOURNALING PROMPTS

- Pick your intentional word or phrase of the day. Think about your week. What can you focus on today that will support your entire week?
  _____

- Can you think of situations this week where you were more in your own A Circle?
  _____
  _____
  _____
  _____

- How was that helpful for you?
  _____
  _____
  _____
  _____

- When you think about your A Circle, can you see how your managing of it can be helpful for your goals? What did you learn this week about how you are able to manage your A Circle?
  _____
  _____
  _____
  _____

- Think of situations in the past that did not go well. An injury? Maybe you broke down under pressure, or you were worried about what people were thinking of you. Write them down.
  _____
  _____
  _____
  _____

- Looking back, do you see that if you would have known these tools and strategies, they would have been helpful? Remember, you did the best you could with what you knew at the time. What strategies could you have used? What could you have had in your A Circle?

    _____
    _____
    _____
    _____
    _____
    _____

- This week, when you look back, name 3 reasons for your success.

    _____
    _____
    _____
    _____

- What do you do well? How do you do it well? Remember: nobody does your skills/sport/game better than you —be confident in that.

    _____
    _____
    _____
    _____
    _____
    _____

- Step back and practice joy. Where do you have the most joy in your life? Do more of that.

    _____
    _____
    _____
    _____
    _____
    _____

I AM SO PROUD OF YOU!

SATURDAY DAILY JOURNALING   DATE _____

CELEBRATION DAY!

- Think of 5 situations where you were successful. Write them down.

_____
_____
_____
_____
_____
_____

- Think of 5 things that you accomplished this week. Write them down.

_____
_____
_____
_____
_____
_____

- Where did you build strength this week mentally? Physically?

_____
_____
_____
_____
_____
_____

- What did you learn from this week that can support you to achieve your goals?

_____
_____
_____
_____
_____
_____

- What went well? What didn't go well? And what can you learn from both?

  _____
  _____
  _____
  _____
  _____
  _____

- Remember that you are not equal to the result. When you accomplish a goal, it is fantastic —*but you are not equal to it*. Learn from it so you can use that experience and same strategy to build success. Where this week can you use this?

  _____
  _____
  _____
  _____
  _____
  _____
  _____

- Also, you are not equal to the mistake, or what did not go well. Separate yourself from those situations so that you can also learn from them. Can you think of any situation this week where you can practice this? Are you hard on yourself? Do you have high expectations of yourself? That's okay, but neither of those things belong in your A Circle when you are doing your sport. Did you have situations this week where this got in your way?

  _____
  _____
  _____
  _____
  _____
  _____
  _____

SUNDAY! DAILY JOURNALING   DATE _____

DREAM DAY!

- Give yourself permission to dream. We need to practice dreaming. It's not a bad thing to desire, or to want things in your life! Putting your best self into your life, sharing your gift to the world, being more of you, is your responsibility and your job. Dreaming only inspires more of you in that way. As you practice putting more of you into your life, you can share that with others; that is inspiring. Where this week were you more of you?

  _____
  _____
  _____
  _____

- Regarding your answer above, were people receptive to it or a little bit threatened?

  _____
  _____

  Remember this: I can only see in you what I have in myself. So, if I don't see you in all your brightness, it's not because something is wrong with you. It is my lack that is the issue. Do not let someone else's inability to see your light dim it. Practice being your light. Practice seeing other's light as well.

- Practice these 5 mindset rules:
  1. Set big, bold, tremendous goals.
  2. Be grateful for everything you have today, and everything you don't have yet.
  3. Be 100% accountable for your life. It doesn't mean that everything is your fault, but taking 100% responsibility for it moves you forward with strength.
  4. Be thankful – for everything that went well and for everything that didn't go well.
  5. Act, speak, think, and perform from the perspective of your Goal Beyond The Goal®.

  Practice these mindset rules EVERY day.

MONDAY DAILY JOURNALING   DATE _____

MENTAL MINDSET FOR THE WEEK

Being triggered by another person's bad behavior means that there is a part of you that needs healing. Continue to stay in your A Circle to support yourself through your reaction to their behavior. Give yourself a new place to land —continue to do your thing, show up for yourself, and don't hold back from being your amazing best self!

JOURNALING PROMPTS

- Pick your intentional word or phrase of the day.
  _____

- Think about the past, what strategies did you use? The Doing Strategy®? The Learning Strategy®? Combination? Both? Neither?
  _____
  _____
  _____
  _____

- Think about what went well and what did not go well in the past. What strategies were you using in those situations? What was in your A Circle?
  _____
  _____
  _____
  _____

- Where do you see yourself in 3 years? You can always change your mind, but think big, think boldly, just explore in lots of different areas of your life.
  _____
  _____
  _____
  _____

- Think about your past — what has been in the way of you being successful? Purge it, write without judgment, move through these things so beyond it you can see the opportunity. Write about the opportunity beyond the struggle.

- Now look at all these things that were in your way. Turn each one around and decide how you can be grateful for each.

TUESDAY DAILY JOURNALING   DATE _____

JOURNALING PROMPTS

- Pick your intentional word or phrase of the day.
  _____

- How did yesterday's intentional word of the day or phrase support you?
  _____
  _____
  _____

- How did you use the Doing Strategy®, Learning Strategy®, and A-Circle®?
  _____
  _____
  _____
  _____
  _____

- Name a couple of examples where now looking back, you were able to use the strategies to move toward your goal.
  _____
  _____
  _____
  _____
  _____

- What went well yesterday?
  _____
  _____
  _____

- Think about the strategy you were using to do that well? What was it?
  _____
  _____
  _____

- Where can you practice that same strategy moving forward?

- How can this strategy help you achieve your goal in the next 3 months?

- Lets talk about difficult situations. Write down examples of situations for you where you felt victimized, or you felt bad, maybe something or someone that made you feel terrible. Just write things down and get them out.

- In these situations what was in your A Circle?

- Now looking back, think about how you could have supported yourself, or taken care of yourself better. What could you have had in your A Circle to support you?

- What inspired you today?

WEDNESDAY DAILY JOURNALING   DATE _____

JOURNALING PROMPTS

○ Pick your intentional word or phrase of the day.
_____

○ How did yesterday's intentional word of the day or phrase support you and shift your mentality?
_____
_____

○ This week, can you think of examples where you were able to just "do" your skills/game/sport? The Doing Strategy®?
_____
_____

○ When you think of the Learning Strategy®, do you like to see your way through your skills/plays/sport? Feel your way through? Talk your way through? Think your way through? Or a combination? Think of a skill/play/situation where you can practice it. What do you want to be focusing on?
_____
_____
_____

○ Can you practice using this strategy moving forward? Where?
_____
_____
_____

○ Think of a time in your past where you felt confident. Explain your experience.
_____
_____
_____

- When you think back to that experience, go back INTO that experience. Now, as you step out of it, how were you confident? Was it something you felt, something you saw, something you said to yourself, something you heard, or a combination?

  _____
  _____
  _____

- Can you practice this strategy moving forward to be more confident?

  _____
  _____

- Think about experiences for you in the past where you were confident. What was in your A Circle?

  _____
  _____

- Remember, your goal is seeking you as much as you are seeking it. Name 3 things that you have been working on this week that are moving you toward your goal.

  _____
  _____
  _____

- Think about your situation. What are some great things about your situation (coaches, team, parents, club/school) that can support you to achieve your goals?

  _____
  _____
  _____
  _____

- Now as you are more aware of these resources, how can you use them more to support you?

  _____
  _____
  _____

THURSDAY DAILY JOURNALING   DATE _____

JOURNALING PROMPTS

○ Pick your intentional word or phrase of the day. Pick something that keeps you aligned with your "goal self." _____

○ Remember that you have a "present self" and a "goal self." Practice stepping out of your "present self" and stepping into your "goal self" more often. Where have you done that? Where can you do it more?

_____
_____
_____
_____

○ Do you have situations where your A Circle gets crowded with negative thoughts or negative energy or negative people? Are you having trouble kicking them out? If you are struggling with negative things in your A Circle, remember that they were once there for a good reason. So think of a situation where something negative would not leave your A Circle. Now ask yourself what that good reason was that it was there in the first place.

_____
_____
_____
_____

○ An example: if you have fear/anxiety/worry in your A Circle, it is only there to help you pay attention, think about what you want to be doing, or reminding you to focus on what you are doing physically. Practice thanking that energy (yes thanking) so you can use it to your advantage. Think of old situations and practice doing this. What could you have done to support you better in the past?

_____
_____
_____
_____

- Think of some goals outside of your sport that you want to achieve. What are they?

- Can you see how these tools and strategies can support you to achieve them? How?

- Can you see how you can use these tools and strategies to support your team? You do not have to do anything extra other than recognize where your teammates are more connected mentally. Acknowledge that for them —that acknowledgment will come back to support you as well. Where could you have done this in the past?

- You can only see in others what you have in yourself. If it is negative, consider working on your own reflection. What are you reflecting out into the world? Where are you not showing up for yourself? How do you want to change that?

FRIDAY DAILY JOURNALING   DATE _____

JOURNALING PROMPTS

- Pick your intentional word or phrase of the day. Think about your week. What can you focus on today that will support your entire week?
  _____

- Can you think of situations this week where you were more in your own A Circle?
  _____
  _____
  _____
  _____

- How was that helpful for you?
  _____
  _____
  _____
  _____

- When you think about your A Circle, can you see how your managing of it can be helpful for your goals? What did you learn this week about how you are able to manage your A Circle?
  _____
  _____
  _____
  _____

- Think of situations in the past that did not go well. An injury? Maybe you broke down under pressure, or you were worried about what people were thinking of you. Write them down.
  _____
  _____
  _____
  _____

- Looking back, do you see that if you would have known these tools and strategies, they would have been helpful? Remember, you did the best you could with what you knew at the time. What strategies could you have used? What could you have had in your A Circle?

  _____
  _____
  _____
  _____
  _____

- This week, when you look back, name 3 reasons for your success.

  _____
  _____
  _____

- What do you do well? How do you do it well? Remember: nobody does your skills/sport/game better than you —be confident in that.

  _____
  _____
  _____
  _____
  _____

- Step back and practice joy. Where do you have the most joy in your life? Do more of that.

  _____
  _____
  _____
  _____
  _____

I AM SO PROUD OF YOU!

SATURDAY DAILY JOURNALING   DATE _____

CELEBRATION DAY!

O Think of 5 situations where you were successful. Write them down.

_____
_____
_____
_____
_____
_____

O Think of 5 things that you accomplished this week. Write them down.

_____
_____
_____
_____
_____
_____

O Where did you build strength this week mentally? Physically?

_____
_____
_____
_____
_____
_____

O What did you learn from this week that can support you to achieve your goals?

_____
_____
_____
_____
_____
_____

- What went well? What didn't go well? And what can you learn from both?

- Remember that you are not equal to the result. When you accomplish a goal, it is fantastic —*but you are not equal to it*. Learn from it so you can use that experience and same strategy to build success. Where this week can you use this?

- Also, you are not equal to the mistake, or what did not go well. Separate yourself from those situations so that you can also learn from them. Can you think of any situation this week where you can practice this? Are you hard on yourself? Do you have high expectations of yourself? That's okay, but neither of those things belong in your A Circle when you are doing your sport. Did you have situations this week where this got in your way?

SUNDAY! DAILY JOURNALING   DATE _____

DREAM DAY!

O Give yourself permission to dream. We need to practice dreaming. It's not a bad thing to desire, or to want things in your life! Putting your best self into your life, sharing your gift to the world, being more of you, is your responsibility and your job. Dreaming only inspires more of you in that way. As you practice putting more of you into your life, you can share that with others; that is inspiring. Where this week were you more of you?

_____
_____
_____
_____
_____

O Regarding your answer above, were people receptive to it or a little bit threatened?

_____
_____
_____

> Remember this: I can only see in you what I have in myself. So, if I don't see you in all your brightness, it's not because something is wrong with you. It is my lack that is the issue. Do not let someone else's inability to see your light dim it. Practice being your light. Practice seeing other's light as well.

O Practice these 5 mindset rules:
   1. Set big, bold, tremendous goals.
   2. Be grateful for everything you have today, and everything you don't have yet.
   3. Be 100% accountable for your life. It doesn't mean that everything is your fault, but taking 100% responsibility for it moves you forward with strength.
   4. Be thankful – for everything that went well and for everything that didn't go well.
   5. Act, speak, think, and perform from the perspective of your Goal Beyond The Goal®.

Practice these mindset rules EVERY day.

MONTH _____ 20 _____

MONDAY	TUESDAY	WEDNESDAY	THURSDAY

NOBODY DOES *YOU* IN YOUR SPORT BETTER THAN YOU.
BE CONFIDENT IN THAT.

© Stacey Herman Goodrich

FRIDAY	SATURDAY	SUNDAY

MONDAY DAILY JOURNALING   DATE _____

MENTAL MINDSET FOR THE WEEK

Are you feeling victimized by your situation? Remember to connect to your "goal self" if your "present self" is caught up in the chaos.

JOURNALING PROMPTS

O Pick your intentional word or phrase of the day.
_____

O Think about the past, what strategies did you use? The Doing Strategy®? The Learning Strategy®? Combination? Both? Neither?
_____
_____
_____
_____
_____

O Think about what went well and what did not go well in the past. What strategies were you using in those situations? What was in your A Circle?
_____
_____
_____
_____

O Where do you see yourself in 3 years? You can always change your mind, but think big, think boldly, just explore in lots of different areas of your life.
_____
_____
_____
_____
_____

- Think about your past — what has been in the way of you being successful? Purge it, write without judgment, move through these things so beyond it you can see the opportunity. Write about the opportunity beyond the struggle.

- Now look at all these things that were in your way. Turn each one around and decide how you can be grateful for each.

TUESDAY DAILY JOURNALING   DATE _____

JOURNALING PROMPTS

- Pick your intentional word or phrase of the day.
  _____

- How did yesterday's intentional word of the day or phrase support you?
  _____
  _____
  _____

- How did you use the Doing Strategy®, Learning Strategy®, and A-Circle®?
  _____
  _____
  _____
  _____
  _____

- Name a couple of examples where now looking back, you were able to use the strategies to move toward your goal.
  _____
  _____
  _____
  _____
  _____

- What went well yesterday?
  _____
  _____
  _____

- Think about the strategy you were using to do that well? What was it?
  _____
  _____

- Where can you practice that same strategy moving forward?

- How can this strategy help you achieve your goal in the next 3 months?

- Lets talk about difficult situations. Write down examples of situations for you where you felt victimized, or you felt bad, maybe something or someone that made you feel terrible. Just write things down and get them out.

- In these situations what was in your A Circle?

- Now looking back, think about how you could have supported yourself, or taken care of yourself better. What could you have had in your A Circle to support you?

- What inspired you today?

WEDNESDAY DAILY JOURNALING   DATE _____

JOURNALING PROMPTS

○ Pick your intentional word or phrase of the day.
_____

○ How did yesterday's intentional word of the day or phrase support you and shift your mentality?
_____
_____

○ This week, can you think of examples where you were able to just "do" your skills/game/sport? The Doing Strategy®?
_____
_____
_____

○ When you think of the Learning Strategy®, do you like to see your way through your skills/plays/sport? Feel your way through? Talk your way through? Think your way through? Or a combination? Think of a skill/play/situation where you can practice it. What do you want to be focusing on?
_____
_____
_____

○ Can you practice using this strategy moving forward? Where?
_____
_____
_____

○ Think of a time in your past where you felt confident. Explain your experience.
_____
_____
_____

- When you think back to that experience, go back INTO that experience. Now, as you step out of it, how were you confident? Was it something you felt, something you saw, something you said to yourself, something you heard, or a combination?

  _____
  _____
  _____
  _____

- Can you practice this strategy moving forward to be more confident?

  _____
  _____

- Think about experiences for you in the past where you were confident. What was in your A Circle?

  _____
  _____

- Remember, your goal is seeking you as much as you are seeking it. Name 3 things that you have been working on this week that are moving you toward your goal.

  _____
  _____
  _____

- Think about your situation. What are some great things about your situation (coaches, team, parents, club/school) that can support you to achieve your goals?

  _____
  _____
  _____
  _____

- Now as you are more aware of these resources, how can you use them more to support you?

  _____
  _____
  _____

THURSDAY DAILY JOURNALING   DATE _____

JOURNALING PROMPTS

- Pick your intentional word or phrase of the day. Pick something that keeps you aligned with your "goal self." _____

- Remember that you have a "present self" and a "goal self." Practice stepping out of your "present self" and stepping into your "goal self" more often. Where have you done that? Where can you do it more?

  _____
  _____
  _____
  _____

- Do you have situations where your A Circle gets crowded with negative thoughts or negative energy or negative people? Are you having trouble kicking them out? If you are struggling with negative things in your A Circle, remember that they were once there for a good reason. So think of a situation where something negative would not leave your A Circle. Now ask yourself what that good reason was that it was there in the first place.

  _____
  _____
  _____
  _____

- An example: if you have fear/anxiety/worry in your A Circle, it is only there to help you pay attention, think about what you want to be doing, or reminding you to focus on what you are doing physically. Practice thanking that energy (yes thanking) so you can use it to your advantage. Think of old situations and practice doing this. What could you have done to support you better in the past?

  _____
  _____
  _____
  _____

- Think of some goals outside of your sport that you want to achieve. What are they?

- Can you see how these tools and strategies can support you to achieve them? How?

- Can you see how you can use these tools and strategies to support your team? You do not have to do anything extra other than recognize where your teammates are more connected mentally. Acknowledge that for them —that acknowledgment will come back to support you as well. Where could you have done this in the past?

- You can only see in others what you have in yourself. If it is negative, consider working on your own reflection. What are you reflecting out into the world? Where are you not showing up for yourself? How do you want to change that?

FRIDAY DAILY JOURNALING   DATE _____

JOURNALING PROMPTS

- Pick your intentional word or phrase of the day. Think about your week. What can you focus on today that will support your entire week?
  _____

- Can you think of situations this week where you were more in your own A Circle?
  _____
  _____
  _____

- How was that helpful for you?
  _____
  _____
  _____

- When you think about your A Circle, can you see how your managing of it can be helpful for your goals? What did you learn this week about how you are able to manage your A Circle?
  _____
  _____
  _____

- Think of situations in the past that did not go well. An injury? Maybe you broke down under pressure, or you were worried about what people were thinking of you. Write them down.
  _____
  _____
  _____

- Looking back, do you see that if you would have known these tools and strategies, they would have been helpful? Remember, you did the best you could with what you knew at the time. What strategies could you have used? What could you have had in your A Circle?

- This week, when you look back, name 3 reasons for your success.

- What do you do well? How do you do it well? Remember: nobody does your skills/sport/game better than you —be confident in that.

- Step back and practice joy. Where do you have the most joy in your life? Do more of that.

I AM SO PROUD OF YOU!

SATURDAY DAILY JOURNALING DATE _____

CELEBRATION DAY!

O Think of 5 situations where you were successful. Write them down.

_____
_____
_____
_____
_____
_____

O Think of 5 things that you accomplished this week. Write them down.

_____
_____
_____
_____
_____
_____

O Where did you build strength this week mentally? Physically?

_____
_____
_____
_____
_____
_____

O What did you learn from this week that can support you to achieve your goals?

_____
_____
_____
_____
_____
_____

- What went well? What didn't go well? And what can you learn from both?

- Remember that you are not equal to the result. When you accomplish a goal, it is fantastic —*but you are not equal to it*. Learn from it so you can use that experience and same strategy to build success. Where this week can you use this?

- Also, you are not equal to the mistake, or what did not go well. Separate yourself from those situations so that you can also learn from them. Can you think of any situation this week where you can practice this? Are you hard on yourself? Do you have high expectations of yourself? That's okay, but neither of those things belong in your A Circle when you are doing your sport. Did you have situations this week where this got in your way?

SUNDAY! DAILY JOURNALING   DATE _____

DREAM DAY!

○ Give yourself permission to dream. We need to practice dreaming. It's not a bad thing to desire, or to want things in your life! Putting your best self into your life, sharing your gift to the world, being more of you, is your responsibility and your job. Dreaming only inspires more of you in that way. As you practice putting more of you into your life, you can share that with others; that is inspiring. Where this week were you more of you?

_____
_____
_____
_____
_____

○ Regarding your answer above, were people receptive to it or a little bit threatened?

_____
_____
_____

Remember this: I can only see in you what I have in myself. So, if I don't see you in all your brightness, it's not because something is wrong with you. It is my lack that is the issue. Do not let someone else's inability to see your light dim it. Practice being your light. Practice seeing other's light as well.

○ Practice these 5 mindset rules:
  1. Set big, bold, tremendous goals.
  2. Be grateful for everything you have today, and everything you don't have yet.
  3. Be 100% accountable for your life. It doesn't mean that everything is your fault, but taking 100% responsibility for it moves you forward with strength.
  4. Be thankful – for everything that went well and for everything that didn't go well.
  5. Act, speak, think, and perform from the perspective of your Goal Beyond The Goal®.

Practice these mindset rules EVERY day.

MONDAY DAILY JOURNALING   DATE _____

MENTAL MINDSET FOR THE WEEK

What's bothering you today? Remember to look inside yourself, instead of outside yourself, for the answer. At the root of every problem lies the solution.

JOURNALING PROMPTS

- Pick your intentional word or phrase of the day.

  _____

- Think about the past, what strategies did you use? The Doing Strategy®? The Learning Strategy®? Combination? Both? Neither?

  _____
  _____
  _____
  _____

- Think about what went well and what did not go well in the past. What strategies were you using in those situations? What was in your A Circle?

  _____
  _____
  _____
  _____

- Where do you see yourself in 3 years? You can always change your mind, but think big, think boldly, just explore in lots of different areas of your life.

  _____
  _____
  _____
  _____
  _____

- Think about your past — what has been in the way of you being successful? Purge it, write without judgment, move through these things so beyond it you can see the opportunity. Write about the opportunity beyond the struggle.

- Now look at all these things that were in your way. Turn each one around and decide how you can be grateful for each.

TUESDAY DAILY JOURNALING   DATE _____

JOURNALING PROMPTS

O Pick your intentional word or phrase of the day.
_____

O How did yesterday's intentional word of the day or phrase support you?
_____
_____
_____

O How did you use the Doing Strategy®, Learning Strategy®, and A-Circle®?
_____
_____
_____
_____

O Name a couple of examples where now looking back, you were able to use the strategies to move toward your goal.
_____
_____
_____
_____

O What went well yesterday?
_____
_____
_____

O Think about the strategy you were using to do that well? What was it?
_____
_____
_____

- Where can you practice that same strategy moving forward?

- How can this strategy help you achieve your goal in the next 3 months?

- Lets talk about difficult situations. Write down examples of situations for you where you felt victimized, or you felt bad, maybe something or someone that made you feel terrible. Just write things down and get them out.

- In these situations what was in your A Circle?

- Now looking back, think about how you could have supported yourself, or taken care of yourself better. What could you have had in your A Circle to support you?

- What inspired you today?

WEDNESDAY DAILY JOURNALING   DATE _____

JOURNALING PROMPTS

O Pick your intentional word or phrase of the day.
_____

O How did yesterday's intentional word of the day or phrase support you and shift your mentality?
_____
_____

O This week, can you think of examples where you were able to just "do" your skills/game/sport? The Doing Strategy®?
_____
_____
_____

O When you think of the Learning Strategy®, do you like to see your way through your skills/plays/sport? Feel your way through? Talk your way through? Think your way through? Or a combination? Think of a skill/play/situation where you can practice it. What do you want to be focusing on?
_____
_____
_____

O Can you practice using this strategy moving forward? Where?
_____
_____
_____

O Think of a time in your past where you felt confident. Explain your experience.
_____
_____
_____

- When you think back to that experience, go back INTO that experience. Now, as you step out of it, how were you confident? Was it something you felt, something you saw, something you said to yourself, something you heard, or a combination?

  _____
  _____
  _____
  _____

- Can you practice this strategy moving forward to be more confident?

  _____
  _____

- Think about experiences for you in the past where you were confident. What was in your A Circle?

  _____
  _____

- Remember, your goal is seeking you as much as you are seeking it. Name 3 things that you have been working on this week that are moving you toward your goal.

  _____
  _____
  _____

- Think about your situation. What are some great things about your situation (coaches, team, parents, club/school) that can support you to achieve your goals?

  _____
  _____
  _____
  _____

- Now as you are more aware of these resources, how can you use them more to support you?

  _____
  _____
  _____

THURSDAY DAILY JOURNALING   DATE _____

JOURNALING PROMPTS

O Pick your intentional word or phrase of the day. Pick something that keeps you aligned with your "goal self." _____

O Remember that you have a "present self" and a "goal self." Practice stepping out of your "present self" and stepping into your "goal self" more often. Where have you done that? Where can you do it more?

_____
_____
_____
_____

O Do you have situations where your A Circle gets crowded with negative thoughts or negative energy or negative people? Are you having trouble kicking them out? If you are struggling with negative things in your A Circle, remember that they were once there for a good reason. So think of a situation where something negative would not leave your A Circle. Now ask yourself what that good reason was that it was there in the first place.

_____
_____
_____
_____

O An example: if you have fear/anxiety/worry in your A Circle, it is only there to help you pay attention, think about what you want to be doing, or reminding you to focus on what you are doing physically. Practice thanking that energy (yes thanking) so you can use it to your advantage. Think of old situations and practice doing this. What could you have done to support you better in the past?

_____
_____
_____
_____

- Think of some goals outside of your sport that you want to achieve. What are they?

- Can you see how these tools and strategies can support you to achieve them? How?

- Can you see how you can use these tools and strategies to support your team? You do not have to do anything extra other than recognize where your teammates are more connected mentally. Acknowledge that for them —that acknowledgment will come back to support you as well. Where could you have done this in the past?

- You can only see in others what you have in yourself. If it is negative, consider working on your own reflection. What are you reflecting out into the world? Where are you not showing up for yourself? How do you want to change that?

FRIDAY DAILY JOURNALING   DATE _____

JOURNALING PROMPTS

- Pick your intentional word or phrase of the day. Think about your week. What can you focus on today that will support your entire week?

  _____

- Can you think of situations this week where you were more in your own A Circle?

- How was that helpful for you?

- When you think about your A Circle, can you see how your managing of it can be helpful for your goals? What did you learn this week about how you are able to manage your A Circle?

- Think of situations in the past that did not go well. An injury? Maybe you broke down under pressure, or you were worried about what people were thinking of you. Write them down.

○ Looking back, do you see that if you would have known these tools and strategies, they would have been helpful? Remember, you did the best you could with what you knew at the time. What strategies could you have used? What could you have had in your A Circle?

_____
_____
_____
_____
_____

○ This week, when you look back, name 3 reasons for your success.

_____
_____
_____
_____

○ What do you do well? How do you do it well? Remember: nobody does your skills/sport/game better than you —be confident in that.

_____
_____
_____
_____
_____
_____

○ Step back and practice joy. Where do you have the most joy in your life? Do more of that.

_____
_____
_____
_____
_____
_____

I AM SO PROUD OF YOU!

SATURDAY DAILY JOURNALING   DATE _____

CELEBRATION DAY!

○ Think of 5 situations where you were successful. Write them down.

_____
_____
_____
_____
_____
_____

○ Think of 5 things that you accomplished this week. Write them down.

_____
_____
_____
_____
_____
_____

○ Where did you build strength this week mentally? Physically?

_____
_____
_____
_____
_____
_____

○ What did you learn from this week that can support you to achieve your goals?

_____
_____
_____
_____
_____
_____

- What went well? What didn't go well? And what can you learn from both?

- Remember that you are not equal to the result. When you accomplish a goal, it is fantastic —*but you are not equal to it.* Learn from it so you can use that experience and same strategy to build success. Where this week can you use this?

- Also, you are not equal to the mistake, or what did not go well. Separate yourself from those situations so that you can also learn from them. Can you think of any situation this week where you can practice this? Are you hard on yourself? Do you have high expectations of yourself? That's okay, but neither of those things belong in your A Circle when you are doing your sport. Did you have situations this week where this got in your way?

SUNDAY! DAILY JOURNALING   DATE _____

DREAM DAY!

- Give yourself permission to dream. We need to practice dreaming. It's not a bad thing to desire, or to want things in your life! Putting your best self into your life, sharing your gift to the world, being more of you, is your responsibility and your job. Dreaming only inspires more of you in that way. As you practice putting more of you into your life, you can share that with others; that is inspiring. Where this week were you more of you?

  _____
  _____
  _____
  _____

- Regarding your answer above, were people receptive to it or a little bit threatened?

  _____
  _____
  _____

  Remember this: I can only see in you what I have in myself. So, if I don't see you in all your brightness, it's not because something is wrong with you. It is my lack that is the issue. Do not let someone else's inability to see your light dim it. Practice being your light. Practice seeing other's light as well.

- Practice these 5 mindset rules:
  1. Set big, bold, tremendous goals.
  2. Be grateful for everything you have today, and everything you don't have yet.
  3. Be 100% accountable for your life. It doesn't mean that everything is your fault, but taking 100% responsibility for it moves you forward with strength.
  4. Be thankful – for everything that went well and for everything that didn't go well.
  5. Act, speak, think, and perform from the perspective of your Goal Beyond The Goal®.

  Practice these mindset rules EVERY day.

MONDAY DAILY JOURNALING   DATE _____

MENTAL MINDSET FOR THE WEEK

Being more of you is what the world needs. Bring it on!

You've almost journaled your way through Book 1. I can't wait for you to see what's next. Time to order Book 2! **www.so-connected.com/books**

JOURNALING PROMPTS

○ Pick your intentional word or phrase of the day.
_____

○ Think about the past, what strategies did you use? The Doing Strategy®? The Learning Strategy®? Combination? Both? Neither?
_____
_____
_____
_____

○ Think about what went well and what did not go well in the past. What strategies were you using in those situations? What was in your A Circle?
_____
_____
_____
_____

○ Where do you see yourself in 3 years? You can always change your mind, but think big, think boldly, just explore in lots of different areas of your life.
_____
_____
_____
_____

- Think about your past — what has been in the way of you being successful? Purge it, write without judgment, move through these things so beyond it you can see the opportunity. Write about the opportunity beyond the struggle.

- Now look at all these things that were in your way. Turn each one around and decide how you can be grateful for each.

TUESDAY DAILY JOURNALING   DATE _____

JOURNALING PROMPTS

○ Pick your intentional word or phrase of the day.
_____

○ How did yesterday's intentional word of the day or phrase support you?
_____
_____
_____

○ How did you use the Doing Strategy®, Learning Strategy®, and A-Circle®?
_____
_____
_____
_____
_____

○ Name a couple of examples where now looking back, you were able to use the strategies to move toward your goal.
_____
_____
_____
_____
_____

○ What went well yesterday?
_____
_____
_____

○ Think about the strategy you were using to do that well? What was it?
_____
_____
_____

- Where can you practice that same strategy moving forward?

_____
_____
_____
_____

- How can this strategy help you achieve your goal in the next 3 months?

_____
_____
_____
_____

- Lets talk about difficult situations. Write down examples of situations for you where you felt victimized, or you felt bad, maybe something or someone that made you feel terrible. Just write things down and get them out.

_____
_____
_____
_____

- In these situations what was in your A Circle?

_____
_____

- Now looking back, think about how you could have supported yourself, or taken care of yourself better. What could you have had in your A Circle to support you?

_____
_____
_____
_____

- What inspired you today?

_____
_____
_____
_____

WEDNESDAY DAILY JOURNALING   DATE _____

JOURNALING PROMPTS

- Pick your intentional word or phrase of the day.
  _____

- How did yesterday's intentional word of the day or phrase support you and shift your mentality?
  _____
  _____

- This week, can you think of examples where you were able to just "do" your skills/game/sport? The Doing Strategy®?
  _____
  _____
  _____

- When you think of the Learning Strategy®, do you like to see your way through your skills/plays/sport? Feel your way through? Talk your way through? Think your way through? Or a combination? Think of a skill/play/situation where you can practice it. What do you want to be focusing on?
  _____
  _____
  _____

- Can you practice using this strategy moving forward? Where?
  _____
  _____
  _____

- Think of a time in your past where you felt confident. Explain your experience.
  _____
  _____
  _____

- When you think back to that experience, go back INTO that experience. Now, as you step out of it, how were you confident? Was it something you felt, something you saw, something you said to yourself, something you heard, or a combination?

  _____
  _____
  _____
  _____

- Can you practice this strategy moving forward to be more confident?

  _____
  _____

- Think about experiences for you in the past where you were confident. What was in your A Circle?

  _____
  _____

- Remember, your goal is seeking you as much as you are seeking it. Name 3 things that you have been working on this week that are moving you toward your goal.

  _____
  _____
  _____

- Think about your situation. What are some great things about your situation (coaches, team, parents, club/school) that can support you to achieve your goals?

  _____
  _____
  _____
  _____

- Now as you are more aware of these resources, how can you use them more to support you?

  _____
  _____
  _____

THURSDAY DAILY JOURNALING   DATE _____

JOURNALING PROMPTS

○ Pick your intentional word or phrase of the day. Pick something that keeps you aligned with your "goal self." _____

○ Remember that you have a "present self" and a "goal self." Practice stepping out of your "present self" and stepping into your "goal self" more often. Where have you done that? Where can you do it more?

_____
_____
_____
_____

○ Do you have situations where your A Circle gets crowded with negative thoughts or negative energy or negative people? Are you having trouble kicking them out? If you are struggling with negative things in your A Circle, remember that they were once there for a good reason. So think of a situation where something negative would not leave your A Circle. Now ask yourself what that good reason was that it was there in the first place.

_____
_____
_____
_____

○ An example: if you have fear/anxiety/worry in your A Circle, it is only there to help you pay attention, think about what you want to be doing, or reminding you to focus on what you are doing physically. Practice thanking that energy (yes thanking) so you can use it to your advantage. Think of old situations and practice doing this. What could you have done to support you better in the past?

_____
_____
_____
_____

- Think of some goals outside of your sport that you want to achieve. What are they?

- Can you see how these tools and strategies can support you to achieve them? How?

- Can you see how you can use these tools and strategies to support your team? You do not have to do anything extra other than recognize where your teammates are more connected mentally. Acknowledge that for them —that acknowledgment will come back to support you as well. Where could you have done this in the past?

- You can only see in others what you have in yourself. If it is negative, consider working on your own reflection. What are you reflecting out into the world? Where are you not showing up for yourself? How do you want to change that?

FRIDAY DAILY JOURNALING   DATE _____

JOURNALING PROMPTS

- Pick your intentional word or phrase of the day. Think about your week. What can you focus on today that will support your entire week?
  _____

- Can you think of situations this week where you were more in your own A Circle?
  _____
  _____
  _____
  _____

- How was that helpful for you?
  _____
  _____
  _____
  _____

- When you think about your A Circle, can you see how your managing of it can be helpful for your goals? What did you learn this week about how you are able to manage your A Circle?
  _____
  _____
  _____
  _____

- Think of situations in the past that did not go well. An injury? Maybe you broke down under pressure, or you were worried about what people were thinking of you. Write them down.
  _____
  _____
  _____
  _____

- Looking back, do you see that if you would have known these tools and strategies, they would have been helpful? Remember, you did the best you could with what you knew at the time. What strategies could you have used? What could you have had in your A Circle?

  _____
  _____
  _____
  _____
  _____

- This week, when you look back, name 3 reasons for your success.

  _____
  _____
  _____
  _____

- What do you do well? How do you do it well? Remember: nobody does your skills/sport/game better than you —be confident in that.

  _____
  _____
  _____
  _____
  _____
  _____

- Step back and practice joy. Where do you have the most joy in your life? Do more of that.

  _____
  _____
  _____
  _____
  _____
  _____

I AM SO PROUD OF YOU!

SATURDAY DAILY JOURNALING DATE _____

CELEBRATION DAY!

- Think of 5 situations where you were successful. Write them down.

  _____
  _____
  _____
  _____
  _____
  _____
  _____

- Think of 5 things that you accomplished this week. Write them down.

  _____
  _____
  _____
  _____
  _____
  _____
  _____

- Where did you build strength this week mentally? Physically?

  _____
  _____
  _____
  _____
  _____
  _____
  _____

- What did you learn from this week that can support you to achieve your goals?

  _____
  _____
  _____
  _____
  _____
  _____
  _____

- What went well? What didn't go well? And what can you learn from both?

- Remember that you are not equal to the result. When you accomplish a goal, it is fantastic —*but you are not equal to it.* Learn from it so you can use that experience and same strategy to build success. Where this week can you use this?

- Also, you are not equal to the mistake, or what did not go well. Separate yourself from those situations so that you can also learn from them. Can you think of any situation this week where you can practice this? Are you hard on yourself? Do you have high expectations of yourself? That's okay, but neither of those things belong in your A Circle when you are doing your sport. Did you have situations this week where this got in your way?

SUNDAY! DAILY JOURNALING   DATE _____

DREAM DAY!

- Give yourself permission to dream. We need to practice dreaming. It's not a bad thing to desire, or to want things in your life! Putting your best self into your life, sharing your gift to the world, being more of you, is your responsibility and your job. Dreaming only inspires more of you in that way. As you practice putting more of you into your life, you can share that with others; that is inspiring. Where this week were you more of you?

  _____
  _____
  _____
  _____
  _____

- Regarding your answer above, were people receptive to it or a little bit threatened?

  _____
  _____
  _____

  Remember this: I can only see in you what I have in myself. So, if I don't see you in all your brightness, it's not because something is wrong with you. It is my lack that is the issue. Do not let someone else's inability to see your light dim it. Practice being your light. Practice seeing other's light as well.

- Practice these 5 mindset rules:
  1. Set big, bold, tremendous goals.
  2. Be grateful for everything you have today, and everything you don't have yet.
  3. Be 100% accountable for your life. It doesn't mean that everything is your fault, but taking 100% responsibility for it moves you forward with strength.
  4. Be thankful – for everything that went well and for everything that didn't go well.
  5. Act, speak, think, and perform from the perspective of your Goal Beyond The Goal®.

  Practice these mindset rules EVERY day.

MONDAY DAILY JOURNALING   DATE _____

MENTAL MINDSET FOR THE WEEK

What makes you happy? Sprinkle it throughout your day.

JOURNALING PROMPTS

○ Pick your intentional word or phrase of the day.

_____

○ Think about the past, what strategies did you use? The Doing Strategy®? The Learning Strategy®? Combination? Both? Neither?

_____

_____

_____

_____

○ Think about what went well and what did not go well in the past. What strategies were you using in those situations? What was in your A Circle?

_____

_____

_____

_____

○ Where do you see yourself in 3 years? You can always change your mind, but think big, think boldly, just explore in lots of different areas of your life.

_____

_____

_____

_____

- Think about your past — what has been in the way of you being successful? Purge it, write without judgment, move through these things so beyond it you can see the opportunity. Write about the opportunity beyond the struggle.

- Now look at all these things that were in your way. Turn each one around and decide how you can be grateful for each.

TUESDAY DAILY JOURNALING   DATE _____

JOURNALING PROMPTS

○ Pick your intentional word or phrase of the day.
_____

○ How did yesterday's intentional word of the day or phrase support you?
_____
_____
_____

○ How did you use the Doing Strategy®, Learning Strategy®, and A-Circle®?
_____
_____
_____
_____

○ Name a couple of examples where now looking back, you were able to use the strategies to move toward your goal.
_____
_____
_____
_____
_____

○ What went well yesterday?
_____
_____
_____

○ Think about the strategy you were using to do that well? What was it?
_____
_____
_____

- Where can you practice that same strategy moving forward?
  _____
  _____
  _____
  _____

- How can this strategy help you achieve your goal in the next 3 months?
  _____
  _____
  _____
  _____

- Lets talk about difficult situations. Write down examples of situations for you where you felt victimized, or you felt bad, maybe something or someone that made you feel terrible. Just write things down and get them out.
  _____
  _____
  _____
  _____

- In these situations what was in your A Circle?
  _____
  _____

- Now looking back, think about how you could have supported yourself, or taken care of yourself better. What could you have had in your A Circle to support you?
  _____
  _____
  _____
  _____

- What inspired you today?
  _____
  _____
  _____
  _____

WEDNESDAY DAILY JOURNALING   DATE _____

JOURNALING PROMPTS

○ Pick your intentional word or phrase of the day.
　_____

○ How did yesterday's intentional word of the day or phrase support you and shift your mentality?
　_____
　_____

○ This week, can you think of examples where you were able to just "do" your skills/game/sport? The Doing Strategy®?
　_____
　_____
　_____

○ When you think of the Learning Strategy®, do you like to see your way through your skills/plays/sport? Feel your way through? Talk your way through? Think your way through? Or a combination? Think of a skill/play/situation where you can practice it. What do you want to be focusing on?
　_____
　_____
　_____

○ Can you practice using this strategy moving forward? Where?
　_____
　_____
　_____

○ Think of a time in your past where you felt confident. Explain your experience.
　_____
　_____
　_____

- When you think back to that experience, go back INTO that experience. Now, as you step out of it, how were you confident? Was it something you felt, something you saw, something you said to yourself, something you heard, or a combination?

- Can you practice this strategy moving forward to be more confident?

- Think about experiences for you in the past where you were confident. What was in your A Circle?

- Remember, your goal is seeking you as much as you are seeking it. Name 3 things that you have been working on this week that are moving you toward your goal.

- Think about your situation. What are some great things about your situation (coaches, team, parents, club/school) that can support you to achieve your goals?

- Now as you are more aware of these resources, how can you use them more to support you?

THURSDAY DAILY JOURNALING   DATE _____

JOURNALING PROMPTS

- Pick your intentional word or phrase of the day. Pick something that keeps you aligned with your "goal self." _____

- Remember that you have a "present self" and a "goal self." Practice stepping out of your "present self" and stepping into your "goal self" more often. Where have you done that? Where can you do it more?

  _____
  _____
  _____
  _____

- Do you have situations where your A Circle gets crowded with negative thoughts or negative energy or negative people? Are you having trouble kicking them out? If you are struggling with negative things in your A Circle, remember that they were once there for a good reason. So think of a situation where something negative would not leave your A Circle. Now ask yourself what that good reason was that it was there in the first place.

  _____
  _____
  _____
  _____

- An example: if you have fear/anxiety/worry in your A Circle, it is only there to help you pay attention, think about what you want to be doing, or reminding you to focus on what you are doing physically. Practice thanking that energy (yes thanking) so you can use it to your advantage. Think of old situations and practice doing this. What could you have done to support you better in the past?

  _____
  _____
  _____
  _____

- Think of some goals outside of your sport that you want to achieve. What are they?

- Can you see how these tools and strategies can support you to achieve them? How?

- Can you see how you can use these tools and strategies to support your team? You do not have to do anything extra other than recognize where your teammates are more connected mentally. Acknowledge that for them —that acknowledgment will come back to support you as well. Where could you have done this in the past?

- You can only see in others what you have in yourself. If it is negative, consider working on your own reflection. What are you reflecting out into the world? Where are you not showing up for yourself? How do you want to change that?

FRIDAY DAILY JOURNALING   DATE _____

JOURNALING PROMPTS

- Pick your intentional word or phrase of the day. Think about your week. What can you focus on today that will support your entire week?
  _____

- Can you think of situations this week where you were more in your own A Circle?
  _____
  _____
  _____
  _____

- How was that helpful for you?
  _____
  _____
  _____
  _____

- When you think about your A Circle, can you see how your managing of it can be helpful for your goals? What did you learn this week about how you are able to manage your A Circle?
  _____
  _____
  _____
  _____

- Think of situations in the past that did not go well. An injury? Maybe you broke down under pressure, or you were worried about what people were thinking of you. Write them down.
  _____
  _____
  _____
  _____

- Looking back, do you see that if you would have known these tools and strategies, they would have been helpful? Remember, you did the best you could with what you knew at the time. What strategies could you have used? What could you have had in your A Circle?

    _____
    _____
    _____
    _____
    _____

- This week, when you look back, name 3 reasons for your success.

    _____
    _____
    _____

- What do you do well? How do you do it well? Remember: nobody does your skills/sport/game better than you —be confident in that.

    _____
    _____
    _____
    _____
    _____

- Step back and practice joy. Where do you have the most joy in your life? Do more of that.

    _____
    _____
    _____
    _____
    _____

I AM SO PROUD OF YOU!

SATURDAY DAILY JOURNALING   DATE _____

CELEBRATION DAY!

- ○ Think of 5 situations where you were successful. Write them down.

  _____
  _____
  _____
  _____
  _____
  _____

- ○ Think of 5 things that you accomplished this week. Write them down.

  _____
  _____
  _____
  _____
  _____
  _____

- ○ Where did you build strength this week mentally? Physically?

  _____
  _____
  _____
  _____
  _____
  _____

- ○ What did you learn from this week that can support you to achieve your goals?

  _____
  _____
  _____
  _____
  _____
  _____

- What went well? What didn't go well? And what can you learn from both?

- Remember that you are not equal to the result. When you accomplish a goal, it is fantastic —*but you are not equal to it*. Learn from it so you can use that experience and same strategy to build success. Where this week can you use this?

- Also, you are not equal to the mistake, or what did not go well. Separate yourself from those situations so that you can also learn from them. Can you think of any situation this week where you can practice this? Are you hard on yourself? Do you have high expectations of yourself? That's okay, but neither of those things belong in your A Circle when you are doing your sport. Did you have situations this week where this got in your way?

SUNDAY! DAILY JOURNALING   DATE _____

DREAM DAY!

○ Give yourself permission to dream. We need to practice dreaming. It's not a bad thing to desire, or to want things in your life! Putting your best self into your life, sharing your gift to the world, being more of you, is your responsibility and your job. Dreaming only inspires more of you in that way. As you practice putting more of you into your life, you can share that with others; that is inspiring. Where this week were you more of you?

_____
_____
_____
_____
_____

○ Regarding your answer above, were people receptive to it or a little bit threatened?

_____
_____
_____

Remember this: I can only see in you what I have in myself. So, if I don't see you in all your brightness, it's not because something is wrong with you. It is my lack that is the issue. Do not let someone else's inability to see your light dim it. Practice being your light. Practice seeing other's light as well.

○ Practice these 5 mindset rules:
1. Set big, bold, tremendous goals.
2. Be grateful for everything you have today, and everything you don't have yet.
3. Be 100% accountable for your life. It doesn't mean that everything is your fault, but taking 100% responsibility for it moves you forward with strength.
4. Be thankful – for everything that went well and for everything that didn't go well.
5. Act, speak, think, and perform from the perspective of your Goal Beyond The Goal®.

Practice these mindset rules EVERY day.

MONDAY DAILY JOURNALING   DATE _____

MENTAL MINDSET FOR THE WEEK

Yes! Congratulations —you are mentally stronger! I am so proud of you!

JOURNALING PROMPTS

○ Pick your intentional word or phrase of the day.
_____

○ Think about the past, what strategies did you use? The Doing Strategy®? The Learning Strategy®? Combination? Both? Neither?
_____
_____
_____
_____

○ Think about what went well and what did not go well in the past. What strategies were you using in those situations? What was in your A Circle?
_____
_____
_____
_____

○ Where do you see yourself in 3 years? You can always change your mind, but think big, think boldly, just explore in lots of different areas of your life.
_____
_____
_____
_____
_____

- Think about your past — what has been in the way of you being successful? Purge it, write without judgment, move through these things so beyond it you can see the opportunity. Write about the opportunity beyond the struggle.

- Now look at all these things that were in your way. Turn each one around and decide how you can be grateful for each.

TUESDAY DAILY JOURNALING   DATE _____

JOURNALING PROMPTS

- Pick your intentional word or phrase of the day.
  _____

- How did yesterday's intentional word of the day or phrase support you?
  _____
  _____
  _____

- How did you use the Doing Strategy®, Learning Strategy®, and A-Circle®?
  _____
  _____
  _____
  _____
  _____

- Name a couple of examples where now looking back, you were able to use the strategies to move toward your goal.
  _____
  _____
  _____
  _____
  _____

- What went well yesterday?
  _____
  _____
  _____

- Think about the strategy you were using to do that well? What was it?
  _____
  _____
  _____

- Where can you practice that same strategy moving forward?

- How can this strategy help you achieve your goal in the next 3 months?

- Lets talk about difficult situations. Write down examples of situations for you where you felt victimized, or you felt bad, maybe something or someone that made you feel terrible. Just write things down and get them out.

- In these situations what was in your A Circle?

- Now looking back, think about how you could have supported yourself, or taken care of yourself better. What could you have had in your A Circle to support you?

- What inspired you today?

WEDNESDAY DAILY JOURNALING   DATE _____

JOURNALING PROMPTS

- Pick your intentional word or phrase of the day.
  _____

- How did yesterday's intentional word of the day or phrase support you and shift your mentality?
  _____
  _____

- This week, can you think of examples where you were able to just "do" your skills/game/sport? The Doing Strategy®?
  _____
  _____
  _____

- When you think of the Learning Strategy®, do you like to see your way through your skills/plays/sport? Feel your way through? Talk your way through? Think your way through? Or a combination? Think of a skill/play/situation where you can practice it. What do you want to be focusing on?
  _____
  _____
  _____

- Can you practice using this strategy moving forward? Where?
  _____
  _____
  _____

- Think of a time in your past where you felt confident. Explain your experience.
  _____
  _____
  _____

- When you think back to that experience, go back INTO that experience. Now, as you step out of it, how were you confident? Was it something you felt, something you saw, something you said to yourself, something you heard, or a combination?

  _____
  _____
  _____

- Can you practice this strategy moving forward to be more confident?

  _____
  _____

- Think about experiences for you in the past where you were confident. What was in your A Circle?

  _____
  _____

- Remember, your goal is seeking you as much as you are seeking it. Name 3 things that you have been working on this week that are moving you toward your goal.

  _____
  _____
  _____

- Think about your situation. What are some great things about your situation (coaches, team, parents, club/school) that can support you to achieve your goals?

  _____
  _____
  _____

- Now as you are more aware of these resources, how can you use them more to support you?

  _____
  _____
  _____

THURSDAY DAILY JOURNALING   DATE _____

JOURNALING PROMPTS

- Pick your intentional word or phrase of the day. Pick something that keeps you aligned with your "goal self." _____

- Remember that you have a "present self" and a "goal self." Practice stepping out of your "present self" and stepping into your "goal self" more often. Where have you done that? Where can you do it more?

  _____
  _____
  _____
  _____

- Do you have situations where your A Circle gets crowded with negative thoughts or negative energy or negative people? Are you having trouble kicking them out? If you are struggling with negative things in your A Circle, remember that they were once there for a good reason. So think of a situation where something negative would not leave your A Circle. Now ask yourself what that good reason was that it was there in the first place.

  _____
  _____
  _____
  _____

- An example: if you have fear/anxiety/worry in your A Circle, it is only there to help you pay attention, think about what you want to be doing, or reminding you to focus on what you are doing physically. Practice thanking that energy (yes thanking) so you can use it to your advantage. Think of old situations and practice doing this. What could you have done to support you better in the past?

  _____
  _____
  _____
  _____

- Think of some goals outside of your sport that you want to achieve. What are they?

- Can you see how these tools and strategies can support you to achieve them? How?

- Can you see how you can use these tools and strategies to support your team? You do not have to do anything extra other than recognize where your teammates are more connected mentally. Acknowledge that for them —that acknowledgment will come back to support you as well. Where could you have done this in the past?

- You can only see in others what you have in yourself. If it is negative, consider working on your own reflection. What are you reflecting out into the world? Where are you not showing up for yourself? How do you want to change that?

FRIDAY DAILY JOURNALING   DATE _____

JOURNALING PROMPTS

- Pick your intentional word or phrase of the day. Think about your week. What can you focus on today that will support your entire week?
  _____

- Can you think of situations this week where you were more in your own A Circle?
  _____
  _____
  _____
  _____

- How was that helpful for you?
  _____
  _____
  _____
  _____

- When you think about your A Circle, can you see how your managing of it can be helpful for your goals? What did you learn this week about how you are able to manage your A Circle?
  _____
  _____
  _____
  _____

- Think of situations in the past that did not go well. An injury? Maybe you broke down under pressure, or you were worried about what people were thinking of you. Write them down.
  _____
  _____
  _____
  _____

- Looking back, do you see that if you would have known these tools and strategies, they would have been helpful? Remember, you did the best you could with what you knew at the time. What strategies could you have used? What could you have had in your A Circle?

  _____
  _____
  _____
  _____
  _____

- This week, when you look back, name 3 reasons for your success.

  _____
  _____
  _____

- What do you do well? How do you do it well? Remember: nobody does your skills/sport/game better than you —be confident in that.

  _____
  _____
  _____
  _____
  _____

- Step back and practice joy. Where do you have the most joy in your life? Do more of that.

  _____
  _____
  _____
  _____
  _____

I AM SO PROUD OF YOU!

SATURDAY DAILY JOURNALING   DATE _____

CELEBRATION DAY!

O Think of 5 situations where you were successful. Write them down.

_____

O Think of 5 things that you accomplished this week. Write them down.

_____

O Where did you build strength this week mentally? Physically?

_____

O What did you learn from this week that can support you to achieve your goals?

_____

- What went well? What didn't go well? And what can you learn from both?

- Remember that you are not equal to the result. When you accomplish a goal, it is fantastic —*but you are not equal to it.* Learn from it so you can use that experience and same strategy to build success. Where this week can you use this?

- Also, you are not equal to the mistake, or what did not go well. Separate yourself from those situations so that you can also learn from them. Can you think of any situation this week where you can practice this? Are you hard on yourself? Do you have high expectations of yourself? That's okay, but neither of those things belong in your A Circle when you are doing your sport. Did you have situations this week where this got in your way?

SUNDAY! DAILY JOURNALING   DATE _____

DREAM DAY!

- Give yourself permission to dream. We need to practice dreaming. It's not a bad thing to desire, or to want things in your life! Putting your best self into your life, sharing your gift to the world, being more of you, is your responsibility and your job. Dreaming only inspires more of you in that way. As you practice putting more of you into your life, you can share that with others; that is inspiring. Where this week were you more of you?

  _____
  _____
  _____
  _____

- Regarding your answer above, were people receptive to it or a little bit threatened?

  _____
  _____
  _____

  Remember this: I can only see in you what I have in myself. So, if I don't see you in all your brightness, it's not because something is wrong with you. It is my lack that is the issue. Do not let someone else's inability to see your light dim it. Practice being your light. Practice seeing other's light as well.

- Practice these 5 mindset rules:
  1. Set big, bold, tremendous goals.
  2. Be grateful for everything you have today, and everything you don't have yet.
  3. Be 100% accountable for your life. It doesn't mean that everything is your fault, but taking 100% responsibility for it moves you forward with strength.
  4. Be thankful – for everything that went well and for everything that didn't go well.
  5. Act, speak, think, and perform from the perspective of your Goal Beyond The Goal®.

  Practice these mindset rules EVERY day.